TIME'S PURPLED MASQUERS

Time's Purpled Masquers

Stars and the Afterlife in
Renaissance English Literature

ALASTAIR FOWLER

CLARENDON PRESS · OXFORD
1996

Oxford University Press, Walton Street, Oxford OX2 6DP
Oxford New York
Athens Auckland Bangkok Bombay
Calcutta Cape Town Dar es Salaam Delhi
Florence Hong Kong Istanbul Karachi
Kuala Lumpur Madras Madrid Melbourne
Mexico City Nairobi Paris Singapore
Taipei Tokyo Toronto
and associated companies in
Berlin Ibadan

Oxford is a trade mark of Oxford University Press

Published in the United States
by Oxford University Press Inc., New York

British Library Cataloguing in Publication Data
Data available

Library of Congress Cataloging in Publication Data
Fowler, Alastair.
Time's purpled masquers: stars and the afterlife in Renaissance
English literature / Alastair Fowler.
Includes bibliographical references and index.
1. English literature—Early modern, 1500–1700—History and
criticism. 2. Astronomy, Renaissance, in literature.
3. Immortality in literature. 4. Future life in literature.
5. Heaven in literature. 6. Renaissance—England. 7. Stars in
literature. 8. Death in literature. 9. Figures of speech.
I. Title.
PR428.A77F69 1996   820.935620   9540023
ISBN 0–19–818340–2

1 3 5 7 9 10 8 6 4 2

Typeset by J&L Composition Ltd, Filey, North Yorkshire
Printed in Great Britain
on acid-free paper by
Biddles Ltd,
Guildford and King's Lynn

Your blazing world beyond the stars mounts higher,
Enlightens all with a celestial fire.

(William Cavendish)

The organs of thy providence divine,
Books ever open, Signs that clearly shine,
Time's purpled Masquers then do them advance,
As by sweet Music in a measured Dance.

(William Drummond, 'An Hymn of the Fairest Fair')

Preface

This book arises from the eight lectures and seminars I gave at the University of Bristol in 1991, as Read-Tuckwell lecturer for that year. The Alice Read-Tuckwell Trust was established to fund lecture courses on human immortality and related matters. Preparing the lectures gave me an opportunity to explore a feature of Renaissance literature which has probably struck every serious student as puzzling at one time or another: namely, the extraordinary prominence of astronomical imagery. That the stars were important astrologically is at best a partial explanation. I am more concerned here with the impact of astronomical discoveries—particularly their implications for stellification, or translation to the stars. Renaissance astronomical imagery is often seen as no more than a literary repercussion of Copernicus, just as stellification is dismissed as hyperbolic flattery. But for some time I have felt sure that other factors were involved. In the Renaissance, purely objective science hardly existed.

My approach is not quite that of a historian of ideas. Instead, I have studied the imagery of fame and consolation, in an attempt to discover their coherence within metaphoric structures. The story of how scientific discoveries forced great changes in the Renaissance world-picture has often been related in scientific terms—the terms of an interested party. Here, I tell a different story, of changes in fantasies that supplied less familiar passages of the world-picture. Not formal theories or formulated beliefs, but interactions of the new science with individual hopes of life after death. Seventeenth-century culture was both religious and materialistic. Far from science replacing religion, the literature of the period seems to show a great variety of negotiated reconciliations of the two. Meanwhile, an urge to survive materially after death is squared with new scientific information. There are extreme swings of opinion, strange temporary solutions. How is ascent from the earth to be achieved? The answers are various. Where Leonardo imagines impossible mechanical wings, and we may think of chemical rocket propulsion, fantasists in the seventeenth century look to a chemic 'vehicle', sanctification, or metamorphosis to angelic sainthood.

Too many scholars and friends have tried to straighten out my ideas of these topics for full acknowledgement to be possible. On theology and science, I owe advice or information to Meg Davies, Norman Kreitman, Jean Moss, and William Wallace; on literary matters, to Anne Barton, and J. Daniel Kinney, and W. Wallace Robson; on the visual art background, to Paul Barolsky, Michael Bury, and David Howarth; on alchemy, to Lyndy Abraham. Above all, I have learned from comments of the staff and students who attended the Read-Tuckwell lectures. And, for imaginative hospitality during the lectureship, I am most grateful to John and Diana Burrow, as well as Christopher Rowe.

Readers of the manuscript at Harvard University Press and the Clarendon Press saved me from a number of errors, and made valuable suggestions, for which I am much in their debt.

Alastair Fowler

University of Virginia

Contents

I

Introduction

. . . Man lives from choice in the framework of his own experience, trapped in his former achievements for generations on end.

(Fernand Braudel, *The Structures of Everyday Life*)

Liberal hopefulness
Regards death as a mere border to an improving picture

(Sir William Empson, 'Ignorance of Death')

In 1618 the great Netherlandish jurist Hugo Grotius, a Remonstrant or moderate Calvinist, proved unacceptably dissident in his theology, so that the Stadtholder Prince Maurits of Nassau had him imprisoned. Sentenced to life imprisonment in Loevestein prison, Grotius was allowed visits from his wife, Marie van Reigersbergh. She would regularly bring him a book-chest, and take it away again refilled with the books he no longer required. One evening the chest went back exceptionally full—not of books but of Grotius himself. The porters complained about its weight: did it contain Arminians? And Marie entered into the joke, conceding that the chest might contain Arminian *books*.[1]

This familiar anecdote itself contains heavy implications. Grotius' free passage might be said to depend on his being categorized as reading-matter—belonging to the (then) privileged realm of learning. Again, if the titles of the books in Grotius' chest were known, one would probably find that many were neither Arminian nor strict Calvinist. Seventeenth-century libraries were still largely medieval in their holdings.[2] Renaissance humanism hid, as it were, in a gothic

[1] Schama (1987: 418); Gellinek (1983: 4); Vreeland (1917).
[2] Jayne (1983); Englander *et al.* (1990); Page (1977); Febvre and Martin (1976).

book-chest. Indeed, Renaissance culture in general may be said to have developed within a medieval matrix that gave it life as well as confined it. One has only to recall the continuing influence of St Augustine, or Nicholas of Cusa, or indeed Aristotle of the Schools, to see that the medieval inheritance, far from being a box of inert 'traditional' texts, was full of vital, seminal ideas.

From the time of Francesco Petrarca (1304–74) to that of Giorgio Vasari (1511–74), many Renaissance Italians strove to distance or reshape, reject or reform, the artistic culture of the recent past. Eventually they learned to call it 'German' or 'gothic'—the term 'medieval' was not yet available[3]—and to deplore its darkness and blindness.[4] Every culture is contained by the framing context it inherits, and has in turn to comprehend and enlarge this. It must change, in part, by bringing into the area of attention (into the picture) ideas previously taken for granted or rejected as heterodox; in part by imposing a new frame of assumptions. As if to express this process physically, many medieval pictures were in the Renaissance literally reframed in antique style. The most sacred images might thus be put into a classical tabernacle frame. And if the central halo of a polyptych rose too high for the new entablature, it was remorselessly cropped.[5] This may seem a very secular thing to do. But it is precisely the meaning of 'secularity' that we need to examine afresh.

In Renaissance secular literature and drama, similar exchanges occurred. The pattern of medieval comedy, it becomes evident, provided structural frames for serious drama of distinctively new types, including even tragedy.[6] Other striking instances come in lyric poetry. Here I am by no means only thinking of the early Tudor 'spiritual parodies' that transformed secular songs into divine poems. Still more illuminating is the lyric poetry generally thought of as most

---

[3] On Renaissance and 17th-century terms for gothic art, see Panofsky (1970: 8, 20, 21); Evelyn (1955: vi. 1–7).

[4] Panofsky (1970: 11); Barolsky (1990: 53 ff. and *passim*).

[5] Newbery *et al.* (1990: 20). [6] Jack (1989); S. Snyder (1979).

distinctively Renaissance: the sonnet literature of passion and individual consciousness. For recent scholarship has revealed that several of the principal sonnet and lyric sequences depended structurally on the liturgy of the Church. They incorporated the structural frames of the Psalter and the calendar; following these not only in sequence and arrangement, but even in numerical proportions. Petrarch's and Spenser's sequences are both arranged calendrically; while many of Shakespeare's sonnets correspond to matching Psalms, as Kenneth Muir and others have shown.[7] In Elizabethan sonnets, madrigals, and lute songs—'For my sweet Saynt some service fit will find'; 'Follow thy saint, follow with accents sweet'—the cult of saints was appropriated.[8] And in the seventeenth century Robert Herrick's *Hesperides* took this tendency to the height of baroque apotheosis. In many poems Herrick relates his 'greeny calendar' of secular saints to the ecclesiastical calendar; promising a kinswoman she will be 'a saint . . . in chief, in this poetic liturgy', and assuring 'Saint Ben' he will be 'writ in my psalter'.[9] As a goldsmith, Herrick would know that sixteenth-century portrait miniatures were often set in the jewelled cases of medieval reliquary lockets. And perhaps he also knew that this need not be thought sacrilege. It might reflect an aspiration. Protestants often spoke of their party, and their intimates, as saints. Milton in a sonnet refers to his second wife as 'my late espousèd saint'. In all these instances, erotic experience was explored in a distinctively Renaissance way; and, in all, human love became a means of symbolizing divine love. Each Eros was likely to have an accompanying Anteros.

We write, as we live, within a frame of past experience that is far from passive or inert. Cultural 'remains' are seldom mere detritus, at least psychologically: more often they are

---

[7] Roche (1989); Muir (1979); Dunlop (1970); Thompson (1985).

[8] Spenser, *Amoretti*, xxii; Thomas Campian: Sternfeld and Greer (1967: 659).

[9] Fowler (1980: 250); among poems in *Hesperides* on the theme of liturgy may be instanced Herrick (1968: 168.1, 169. 3, 188. 1, 188. 4, 199.1). Some remembered, perhaps, that St Chrystostom had called a lady friend 'saint'.

very active.[10] The past may interrogate the present, just as the present the past. In the Renaissance, certainly, innovations were likely to be comprehensively interrogated (if not suppressed) by surviving medieval institutions and mental habits. Yet survivals, more positively, might also challenge revaluation or encourage visionary aspirations.

Renaissance and Reformation

Only to a superficial view does the Renaissance seem a beginning *de novo* or *all' antico*. More substantially, it continued a process traceable deep into the Middle Ages—to the twelfth century and beyond. As Erwin Panofsky argued in his seminal study, renaissance intermittently recurred, over a long period, as a movement of alternating phases.[11] At first unquestionably posited on dominance of the Christian religion, it was a drive for reform, an attempt—in the suggestive phrase of a recent historian—to 'resurrect the Church'.[12] Later, *renascità* ('rebirth') was an idea closely associated, in Reformed theology, with the baptism of repentance. Seroux d'Agincourt recoined the term 'Renaissance' in the nineteenth century to refer specifically to the recovery of classical high culture. But to more recent historians, as to the generation of Giorgio Vasari, it has signified a great deal more than that.[13] To Pierre Belon in 1553—and earlier, to Petrarch and to Leon Battista Alberti—the 'desirable renaissance' of *bonnes disciplines* from out of the darkness and sleep of ignorance was unmistakably a religious awakening.[14] The 'ruins of Rome' obsessively meditated by Renaissance poets and artists—Petrarch and Du Bellay, Spenser and Shakespeare, Jan Sadeler and Maarten van Heemskerck—were signs neither of pagan supersession nor, merely, of papal decline; instead, they repre-

---

[10] Jung (1968: 262).   [11] Panofsky (1970); Onians (1988).
[12] Wright (1982); Bossy (1985); Greene (1982, chs. 2 and 3).
[13] W. Kerrigan and G. Braden (1989: 9). On the myth of the Renaissance, see Bullen (1994).   [14] Panofsky (1970: 17).

sented surviving links with virtuous antiquity.[15] The literal
rediscovery of ancient Rome by excavation, which so excited
Petrarch, symbolized nothing less than the restauration of
cultural forms free from the corruptions of the recently
degenerate world above ground. His imperial vision,
prompted by the archaeological remains of ancient Rome,
one should not forget, is immediately preceded, and motivated, by an equally excited catalogue of Rome's pious relics
and ecclesiastical antiquities.[16] For Petrarch, antiquities seem
to have amounted almost to *vestigiae naturae*, traces of pristine
nature. One recalls that for Spenser, Camden showed 'the
light of simple veritie, | Buried in ruines',[17] and that Francis
Bacon, on viewing the Earl of Arundel's collection of ancient
marbles, paid the revealing compliment 'I see the resurrection
is upon us.'[18] In the Renaissance, hyperbolic claims for art,
however aestheticist they may seem now, were likely to be
expressed through religious imagery, if not to cover real
religious hopes. A common portrait type showed the sitter
(often a humanist collector) with hand on a sculpted beast;
where the collector was also a sculptor, the design implied that
the sculpture would outlast its author. But such portraits have
been shown to derive from a *vanitas* type in which the sitter's
hand held a skull.[19]

Central to any adequate understanding of the Renaissance
must be the thrust of humanist learning. My assumption in
what follows is that the recovery of ancient learning—pagan

[15] Greene (1982); Hieatt (1983). Countless prints by Jan Sadeler, Hieronymus
Cock, Maarten van Heemskerck, and others witness to the fascination of
classical ruins. Sadeler is particularly interested in traces of ancient cults—
idols, altars, and ceremonies surviving in rustic customs.

[16] *Familiar Epistles*, IX. xiii: cit. Greene (1982: 88–9), where the previous
paragraph, however, is passed over. Cf. *Familar Epistles*, I. v, where Cologne,
city of the Magi and of peace, is contrasted with present-day Rome, city of
'imperial' military power.   [17] *Ruines of Time*, lines 171–2.

[18] Howarth (1985: 53).

[19] Held (1969: 25–8); Filipczak (1987: 111). In the 17th century, this iconographical development was sometimes reversed. In the final version of Robert
Walker's famous portrait of John Evelyn (National Portrait Gallery, London),
a collector's item is replaced by a skull.

as well as patristic—aimed to reverse the most recent of medieval declines. It was the hope of many that through improved learning religion would be reformed and society come to consist of reborn individuals. (They can hardly have foreseen that individualistic reform would leave the power of the state not only unchecked but greater than ever.[20]) In humanism's earlier phases, pagan and Christian learning joined hands to promote a *pietas litterata*—often innocent of any sense of impropriety. One thinks of the serene balance of classical and Christian figures in the Studiolo at Urbino, or the 'poetic religion' whereby poets from Petrarch to Spenser addressed solemn mysteries of theology through pagan mythological imagery.[21] The relaxed composure of such syntheses should not be altogether surprising. Humanism began, after all, in a monastic context, under the aegis of devout figures like the Abbot Trithemius, while several northern humanists, notably Erasmus and Colet, were also reformers.[22]

Erasmus was careful to point out that the Christian culture had developed out of the Greek, that the best of the Fathers had derived much of their learning from pagan philosophy and that the very structure of Christian dogma was not exempt from the influence of pagan thought . . . the ancients, or at least the best of them, taught an ethic as near as makes no matter to the Christian. . . . The best of their culture led up to it and was therefore in harmony with its dictates.[23]

Only later—and especially after the Council of Trent—came the suspicion of learning, the suppression of careless syncretism, the restriction of Hebrew studies, the persecution of heresy. But, however powerful the reaction in Italy and Spain, it should not be regarded as typical of Christians even there. Everywhere, indeed, even in universities, the

[20] Bossy (1985: 124–5).
[21] Cheles (1986: 13); Minnis (1982); Trinkaus (1983); Wind (1967).
[22] Bolgar (1954, index, s.v. *pietas litterata*); Brann (1981); Boyle (1981); Cesareo (1990); Southern (1994).   [23] Bolgar (1954: 337).

theme was still reform. And Reformation and Counter-Reformation theologians alike appealed to the authority of the early Latin Fathers and (especially in the seventeenth century) of the still more pristine Greek Fathers, with all the difficult learning that entailed. The challenge of St Augustine was felt throughout Europe.

Even where the visual arts were concerned, one finds the emphasis on reform—to an extent that nineteenth-century historians hardly did justice to. Giorgio Vasari, in particular, frequently describes the Middle Ages as a time of 'the deepest debasement' for the arts: 'After the departure of Constantine . . . not only sculpture, but painting and architecture, fell constantly from bad to worse, and this, perhaps, because human affairs, when they begin to decline, never cease to sink, until they have reached the lowest depths of deterioration.'[24] In Vasari's Life of Cimabue, the Middle Ages become a Fall: the ancients, pagan as they were, he thinks of as almost prelapsarian; being nearer to the first origin of the arts in uncorrupted nature. The subject of the *Lives of the Artists* is proposed as the arts' 'restoration, or rather second birth'. No mere tactic of disarming the repressive authorities could possibly have produced the consistent vision with which Vasari conceives this renewal in terms of Christian reformation and mission; the *Lives of the Artists* are modelled throughout on the lives of the saints.[25] It was hardly caution that led Vasari to affirm that Michelangelo (whom W. E. H. Lecky calls 'the chief agent in the secularization of painting'[26]) was 'sent by God'.[27]

Vasari's religious view of the Renaissance is unusually explicit and articulate, but not totally uncharacteristic of his time. The discovery of Tullia's unextinguished lamp; Petrarch's imagined repeopling of the ruins of Rome; Michelangelo's excavation of a *sleeping* Eros: these and many similar

[24] Vasari (1901: 19).   [25] Cf. Barolsky (1990: 53–4, 56).
[26] Cit. Haskell (1993: 407).
[27] Vasari (1901, pref. to pt. II); cf. Burke (1987*b*, s.v. *Rinascimento*).

incidents typify a period when continuity with the ancient world was almost an article of religion. Regeneration was to bring back ancient civilization; civilization would restore the 'high perfection' of the prelapsarian world. Considering these ideas, it comes to seem almost inevitable that Vasari should have cast his biographies of artists, however unsuitably at times, in the mould of saints' lives.[28] His Academy of Design is churchlike, his artists saints or pilgrims.[29] Allowance must of course be made for the desire to improve the status of the visual arts, as well as for the limiting pressures of the generic forms available. None the less, the reforming tenor of Vasari's *Lives* is striking enough.

Historians used to engage in exquisite determinations of precisely when Renaissance might be said to have begun to turn to Reformation (or Counter-Reformation). They could have saved much effort by identifying the Renaissance as itself a reformation. Petrarch's anti-papal satires, Masaccio's *Trinity*, Leonardo's *Last Supper*: such instances of religious commitment now seem obvious enough. But what of the pagan Renaissance? What of Ovid? The dominating place of the *Metamorphoses* in sixteenth-century literature—and even more, perhaps, in visual art—should by no means be thought of as a counter-instance. Instead, it vividly illustrates the importance accorded to personal transformation or regeneration. After centuries of pious allegorizing—after the *Ovide Moralisé* and the *Metamorphosis Ovidiana Moraliter Explanata*[30]—the witty poet's metamorphoses had come to symbolize *passages* to a changed state, a new life.[31] Titian's *Flaying of Marsyas* (to go no further) serves as a good example of the profundity that could still be arrived at through Ovid's stories in the Renaissance.[32] And such Ovidian material scarcely represented antiquity's

[28] Barolsky (1990). Cf. Filippo Baldinucci's Lives, and see R. and M. Wittkower (1963).   [29] Barolsky (1990: 53–4, 56, 62–3).

[30] Anon. (1920); Bersuire (1511).

[31] Bate (1989); Martindale (1988); R. Wittkower (1977: 129–42).

[32] Wind (1967: 171 ff., 188). Raphael, Giulio Romano, and many others painted the flaying of Marsyas; for the literature, see Biadene (1990: 370–2).

highest challenges. Jonson in his *Poetaster* (1600–1) found a reforming model in Augustan culture; and in the renewed classicism of the Restoration a similar ideal was further generalized, morally as well as aesthetically.[33]

In calling the Renaissance a reformation, I have no wish to minimize conflicts of sacred and secular, nor to reduce history to an uninterrupted flow—as if its ruptures were continuities not understood. Still less, to deny the Renaissance ever happened.[34] On the contrary, I shall argue that it was a deeper and more marvellous change than any mere switch of ideology or set of new ideas. Long prepared, long worked for over centuries, the Renaissance renewed learning, reformed religion, attempted a political *renovatio*, achieved a *restauratio*[35] of science, and carried through a comprehensive agricultural revolution, all as parts of a single transformation (although at diverse times in different countries). It was a quantum jump to more conscious, aspiring, so to say excited, states of mind. And if this is anything like the truth, it cannot be appropriate to describe the Renaissance as a secular movement, or as desacralization. Such simplification will hardly bring understanding of the changed consciousness of that remarkable age when modern attitudes to life and death were formed. It cannot do justice, even, to the complex interplay of sacred and profane in early modern culture.

Desacralization

In the late Middle Ages reliquaries containing sacred remains began to be given windows: to frame, to present, their contents visibly. This innovation refuses simple explanation. It may have implied attitudes more sensationalist, or more literalistic, or more individualistic, or more fervent, or more

---

[33] *Poetaster*, I. i, and 'To the Reader', lines 98–107: Herford and Simpson (1925–52: iv. 320). On the phases of Augustanism, see Erskine-Hill (1983).

[34] The implication, almost, of Tillyard (1960).

[35] A Baconian but originally religious term meaning restoration to a pristine state of innocence; cf. Aubrey (1972: 22).

sceptical—or all at once.[36] And perhaps Renaissance motivation was comparably elusive, ambiguous, and complex. At the very least, one needs to enquire, with as few preconceptions as possible, how far the Renaissance was a movement of increasing secularity. Is it sometimes to be interpreted, instead, as an implementation of doctrine, or a revitalizing of nominal beliefs, or a determination to judge religion by its fruits? Historians now broadly agree in rejecting the notion of the Middle Ages as the 'age of faith'. The 'problem of unbelief in the sixteenth century' (the title of Lucien Febvre's study) was an inherited problem, not a new one. And the seventeenth century brought a continuation or recrudescence of superstition and magic: at least as late as 1632 the 'clerical proletariat'[37] were saying charms over pigs. All the same, the Renaissance had happened and continued to happen. Only, its happening was not always in spite of magic and belief: quite often it happened in pursuit of them.

The comparatively recent notion that the Renaissance desacralized found support in the undeniable fact that nature was then comprehensively revalued. On the strength of this, might not natural science be said to have 'displaced religion' in the seventeenth century?[38] The simple answer today would have to be No. There is now more suspicion of the historiographic model valorizing such scientistic claims. ('Displace' implies a Darwinian cultural struggle that never occurred, besides belonging to a hydrostatic analogy—characteristic of Freudian myth-making—that relied for its persuasive effect on bodily fluids being a taboo subject, heavy with significance.) Yet relics of positivism continue to weaken Renaissance studies, in which the place assigned to religion is absurdly inadequate.[39] One is tempted to counter with the assertion

[36] See Bessard (1990: 128).

[37] Wright's phrase; see Thomas (1988: 328). This instance may also serve as a reminder of the time-lags in cultural changes between different ranks and intellectual cadres.   [38] The assumption of R. S. Westfall (1973).

[39] In a sense this is true even of so fine an account as W. Kerrigan and G. Braden (1989); except that it is primarily concerned with 19th-century ideas of the Renaissance.

that, far from 'displacing' religion, early science extended it. Science (which is now more likely to imitate science fiction) in the Renaissance imitated theology.

The Renaissance needs to be reimagined in terms appropriate to the late twentieth century. And this surely involves reconsidering the relation of the former sacred and the profane—the *raison d'être*, if one may so put it, of secularity. Even when religion is renounced, its functions have to be reassigned. Hence, in part, the problematic activity of 'rewriting the Renaissance' in the USA, where scientism and religion coexist uncomfortably.

There are many suggestive (but also distracting) resemblances between our own age and the early modern period, when the pressures and upheavals of reform movements led to fragmentation of Christian doctrine. In theological terms, one might describe the millenarians and other sectaries as seizing, in their various heresies, on the Spirit of Christ, while it was Christ the creative Logos who occupied the thoughts of scientists and 'Christian philosophers'.[40] Orthodox theologians held together two doctrinal emphases: on Christ the individual's redeemer, and on God the Creator. To the latter doctrine, the rise of science may be thought of as responding—again, at times, with heretical results.

Interest in created nature stirred many Renaissance Christians with renewed intensity. John Calvin's energetic restatement of Augustinian ideas is not atypical. The ingratitude of men is shameful, he writes, seeing that

they have in their own persons a factory where innumerable operations of God are carried on, and a magazine stored with treasures of inestimable value . . . their own experience tells them of the vast variety of gifts which they owe to his liberality. . . . The swift and versatile movements of the soul in glancing from heaven to Earth, connecting the future with the past, retaining the remembrance of former years, nay, forming creations of its own—its skill, moreover, in making astonishing discoveries, and inventing so many

[40] As Williams (1962) minutely traces.

wonderful arts, are sure indications of the agency of God in man. (*Institutes of the Christian Religion*)[41]

Such ideas remained characteristic of Calvinism until its impoverishment under puritanism. For Calvinism was far from being the theology of extreme Reformers only; indeed, it was the official doctrine of the Elizabethan settlement.[42] As we shall see, scientific interests were not specially Protestant, let alone Puritan (except for a close association of Calvinism and Copernicanism in Holland). Modern science had begun long before the Reformation, under monastic, private, and even university auspices. Certainly its progress was at first very slow. But the increased activity during the Renaissance in all the sciences—from astronomy and psychology to botany and mineralogy—was a cumulative rather than sudden development. To see how gradually and hesitantly science and art emerged from their religious matrices, one has only to consider the development of still-life painting. Its divergence from ecclesiastical art, particularly manuscript illumination, illustrates perfectly the ambiguity of the new 'secular' interest in natural science.

Framing the Middle Ages

In illuminated manuscripts of the Middle Ages (and still in the London Pliny of about 1460), historiated initials often spread out into a labyrinthine interlace of monstrous vegetable or animal forms, which not only enclose the letter itself but sprawl down the margin, as if to frame the entire page. Such interlace has been compared to the protective labyrinths surrounding ancient temples, to ensure that the initiate's approach was suitably hesitant. Others compare the demonic forms that infested the monastic mind. Or else, the interlace is abstract ornament, meaningless arabesque. Doubtless its functions varied. But the most promising avenue of explana-

[41] I. v. 4–5: Calvin (1949: 53–4).   [42] See Trevor-Roper (1987).

tion is to connect the persistent ingestion by imaginary forms with the *ruminatio* of meditation.[43] The windings of interlace may have suggested divagations of memory, and so have helped to draw readers through associative recollection back to the sacred text. And one can see other grotesqueries as similarly encouraging memory-art—like the marginal jewels that implied certain manuscripts' value as memorial shrines.[44] Perhaps few marginal drolleries were quite without relevance. Grotesque imagery and obscene punning on the text belonged to the memory-art of utilizing libidinal associations.[45]

In fifteenth-century illuminated manuscripts, especially in the Netherlands, the flora and fauna of framing borders become objects of naturalistic interest in a new way.[46] The Delft masters, such as the Master of the Adair Hours, make their shimmering gold or fantastic margins more distinct than before; and often these borders (as one has now to call them) are themselves 'framed' or compartmented off from the central register. The Master of the Dark Eyes and the Master of the Suffrages use tinted panels.[47] The borders may constitute, in effect, flat frames; or else architectural structures (like those of the London Pliny Master) that claim attention as independent objects of interest.[48] When text is enclosed, its spatial whereabouts becomes ambiguous.[49] Thus, it may appear on a suspended sheet intervening somewhere between the viewer and the antique world represented by the monumental architecture. Where the central register contains a sacred image, the border functions as a window-frame. It no longer alludes to the central themes in the

[43] Camille (1992: 64). [44] Carruthers (1990: 41).
[45] Carruthers (1990). This is not to deny the validity of Camille's approach. The same image could fulfil several distinct functions.
[46] Millard Meiss sees the heavier borders of miniatures as motivated by a desire to balance increased recession: Meiss (1969: i. 258).
[47] Marrow *et al.* (1990, sect. 11).
[48] Armstrong (1981); Camille (1992: 154).
[49] e.g. the Master of the Putti, Armstrong (1981: 20).

medieval fashion—not even by parodying or subverting the holy words. Instead, the shallow space of the new borders displays accurate natural histories, or fully realized images of butterflies, flowers, pretzels, biscuits, coins, plaques, in a way that almost inevitably calls to mind the still lifes of a later period. The pea-pods of the Hours of Catherine of Cleves and the molluscs of the Walters Hours are familiar examples.[50]

Such iconically realized objects related to the sacred images or texts within the border in ways that invite enquiry. Sometimes—as with pilgrimage plaques and shells round the margin—one may infer a relation of liminality, of transitionary access from the ordinary space beyond the book. So, too, the saints in the wings of an altar-piece serve as presenters of the central image;[51] and early picture-frames become more explicitly sacred in their decoration inwards, towards the sight edge.[52] On the other hand, Anton Wierix (Antwerp, c.1552–c.1624) can give the Entombment a border of thistle, hollyhock, and other plants, with only a few sheep-bones to suggest the Agnus Dei or the idea of sacrifice. Some of the new border images were still, indeed, familiar symbols of memory-art. Coins invite deposit in the treasure-chest of memory, like the numbered peas in their pod-purses; biscuits ('twice concocted') are for inward digestion; and flowers may represent virtues to be acquired through meditation. The fish and hooks of the Hours of Catherine of Cleves have already been noticed by Mary Carruthers.[53] But explanations in terms of function (or of 'commodification', in the case of Norman Bryson) overlook the sheer interest of the marginal images. These well-observed objects give pleasure by their richly

[50] See Randall (1974), with several illustrations.

[51] For intermediate saints, see e.g. Zafran (1988, no. 3). For frames growing holier towards the sight edge, cf. Newbery et al. (1990: 34); Wieck (1988, fig. 75).

[52] e.g. the late gothic Sienese *cassetta* frame of a Paolo di Giovanni Fei *Madonna and Child Enthroned* in the Metropolitan Museum, illus. Newbery et al. (1990, no. 2), where *pastiglia* leaf-and-vine frames Solomonic columns with images of the Annunciation within octofoil medallions.

[53] Marrow et al. (1990); Carruthers (1990: 246, 345).

detailed realization: they belong to an exterior natural world conceived as attracting the viewer to spiritual joys and meanings within.

Flower-pieces and still lifes, too, had an origin in framing conventions. Late medieval altar-pieces sometimes had still lifes painted on the reverse; so that when the polyptych was closed they formed the outside, the container, for the sacred image within.[54] A symbolic still life, like the niche with ewer, basin, and towel in the exterior of the upper register of Jan van Eyck's Ghent Polyptych (1430), would often be the subject of a whole panel.[55] Even so, subordination to the sacred scheme is sometimes said to have retarded the development of naturalism. That is to mistake matrix for hindrance. After all, Renaissance still life had its origins in Church art—in details of panel paintings (for example, kitchen scenes at the House of Martha and Mary), in murals such as Taddeo Gaddi's fictive niches in the Baroncelli Chapel (*c.*1328–30),[56] in Zurbarán's and Cotán's symbolic still lifes for monastic patrons, in *trompe-l'œil* reverses of Annunciations, and in domestic interiors of the Annunciations themselves. In the seventeenth century, certainly, independent flower- and fruit-pieces became a major product of the Netherlands, with something like 30,000 artists on the assembly-line. And art historians have learnt to be cautious about finding a *vanitas* theme in every fruit-fly. Even so, it remains unclear just how desacralized these 'secular' still lifes were. When flowers could symbolize virtues, their composure in a vase might describe formation of the soul, or the seasons' calendrical plenitude.[57]

In a common type of devotional still life, suggestive for our present enquiry, realistic flowers garland a mandorla, or surround a niche or window framing a religious subject. Jan

[54] Cf. the *vanitas* still lifes on the back of portraits; e.g. the portrait of Jane-Loyse Tissier by Barthel Bruyn the Elder (1493–1555): Schneider (1990: 22).

[55] Kuile (1985: 22). [56] Ladis (1982: 97. 4*a*. 12).

[57] Wind (1967: 268 n.). For more metaphysical implications of the vase of flowers, see Wind (1967: 129–30, 265). As is well known, flowers painted together in Netherlandish flower-pieces often did not in fact bloom simultaneously.

Brueghel II (Antwerp 1601–78) painted several such still lifes with Madonnas, like the *Madonna and Child in a Floral Garland*, with its astonishing collection of 130 flower species.[58] Similarly, the Kassa *Garland of Flowers Around the Holy Family*, probably by Jan Anton van der Baren (1615–86) and Nicolaes van Hoy (1631–79), features minutely observed blooms around a window, through which appears a carpenter's shop; the interior, equally naturalistic and equally devout, has such individual details as minimalist haloes and an angel with a broom.[59] In these garlanded paintings, van der Baren is thought to have followed Daniel Seghers (Antwerp, 1590–1661). The fruit and flowers come near to stealing the show in garlanded pieces by Seghers himself: his Princeton *Rubens Memorial* almost obscures the dead painter's vaguely sculpted, half-visible bust behind abundance of flowers—so lively they seem less to sermonize on mutability than to overgrow death's dim borders with their profuse new life.[60] They leave death no room, as if anticipating Wittgenstein's 'death is not an event of life'.

Fifteenth-century botanical illuminations, sixteenth-century *blumpots*, seventeenth-century garlanded images: all were phases in a single, long-term transformation. In this metamorphosis, picture and border, image of grace and natural setting, meaning and object engage in gradual interchanges— if not to change places in actual fact. Their fields of interest and value interfuse, become diffused one into the other, until mutual interpenetration is complete. The natural verge, perhaps, appropriates the sacred symbols, assimilating significance to the point of offering independently meaningful symbols. The medieval Mirror of Nature was already meaningful. But its meanings were often automatic associations, assigned perfunctorily. Material objects and sense impressions

---

[58] See Freedberg (1981). Cf. e.g. Hendrick van Balen, private coll., illus. Welu (1983); Jan Brueghel de Velours, *The Madonna of the Flowers*. See Ertz (1984, no. 293 and colourplate 60).   [59] Ember (1989: 46).

[60] Cf. Seghers's Mauritshuis *Garland of Flowers Around a Statue of the Virgin*, and J. P. van Thielen's *Flower Garland Round a Bust of Flora* at the Rijksmuseum.

were at best adjuncts to edification—stepping-stones to be passed over as quickly as possible in the rush to allegory. The seventeenth century, by contrast, is an age of natural science, of moralized landscape, of natural images challenging prolonged meditation, of Jakob Boehme's *Signatura Rerum* (translated 1651).[61] Attention can now focus on the physical details of things.[62]

All this needs qualification, of course—for example, by taking into account the Cistercian tradition of landscape meditation. Moreover, images could be rejected, as well as affirmed. The Reformation followed previous reformations in attempting to overcome by destruction the inertia of the past. Recrudescences of philistine iconoclasm occurred everywhere—in Italy as well as in the north. (In the Netherlands, after the iconoclastic fury of 1566, artists retaliated by finding an image for the iconoclasts themselves: the donkey-headed vandals to be seen in the background of several Antwerp gallery paintings.) Representations of nature had to be achieved in the face of condemnations of art's links with unreformed religion.[63] It was nevertheless irrepressible. One might find an apt metaphor of this in the many English illuminated manuscripts nearly destroyed at the dissolution of the monastic houses, which were instead bought up cheaply by Netherlandish booksellers; for these rejected images were later to return in the shape of a copious flood of emblem literature. (Although the decently rational black-and-white of printed emblems mostly lacked the shading to make it an imaginative substitute for colour.) Seventeenth-century emblems sometimes refreshed the images of the old religion, as in Henry Hawkins's *Partheneia Sacra* (1633); or 'corrected' them, as in Francis Quarles's rearrangement of *Pia Desideria*

---

[61] Vergara (1982: 159–66).

[62] Emblems may nevertheless be said to short-circuit a fully receptive observation of nature: see A. B. Howard (1972: 384) on Edward Taylor, and cf. Gilman (1989: 59–60).

[63] Gilman (1986); Filipczak (1987); Feld (1990); Verdon and Henderson (1990); Haigh (1993).

(Antwerp, 1624) by the Jesuit Herman Hugo. Meanwhile, as engagement with natural science intensified, the illuminator's skills were brought to bear on the emergent science of microscopy, by artists like the Hoefnagels, who produced a new kind of book displaying fully detailed insects as if they were profound *symbola* or sacred images.[64]

Renaissance Insets

Interest in microscopy spread far beyond the immediate circles of such scientists as Christiaan Huygens and Robert Hooke. An enthusiasm of virtuosos, it probably did much to encourage the fashion for poems about small creatures. In assessing the swarms of Renaissance grasshopper poems and flea poems, one should remember that Galileo used his lenses to observe not only stars but 'flies which look as big as a lamb, are covered all over with hair, and have very pointed nails',[65] and that it was the prominent Paracelsian physician and naturalist Thomas Moffet (or Mouffet) who wrote *The Silkworms and their Flies* (1599).[66] Microscopy's revelation of a new world, a finely worked, 'artificial' creation—framed within the gross, familiar, old one—gave new meaning to the pious motto *Ex minimis patet ipse Deus*,[67] and may also have had much to do with the baroque aesthetic of *multum in parvo*. (For this was very different from the aesthetic governing the ordinarily proportioned detail of, say, Jan van Eyck.[68]) Thus,

[64] Kuile (1985: 29).
[65] Crombie (1961: ii. 253). Among influential poems on small creatures may be mentioned *Anacreontea*, XXXIV; the medieval *Carmen de Pulice* attributed to Ovid; Sarbiewski's 'Ad Cicadam' (*Lyricorum*, IV. xxiii); Lovelace's 'The Grasshopper'. See Peacham (1906: 75); Donne (1965: 174); D. C. Allen (1968: 152–64); J. Kerrigan (1988: 324). In England, the vogue for compressed poems on small creatures may have been a Caroline, not a Jacobean, literary phenomenon, as Kerrigan thinks. But *La Puce de Madame Des Roches* (1582) was a collection of more than fifty poems on fleas.   [66] Trevor-Roper (1985, index, s.v. *Muffet*).
[67] Sutton *et al.* (1987: 13 and fig. 7).   [68] Cf. Haskell (1993: 480–1).

Richard Leigh (1650–1728), a country doctor and old-fashioned Restoration poet, marvels at

> Nature, who with like State, and equal Pride,
> Her Great Works does in Height and Distance hide,
> And shuts up her Minuter Bodies all
> In curious frames, imperceptibly small.
>
> .   .   .   .
>
> What Skill is in the frame of Insects shown!
> How fine the threds, in their small Textures spun!
> How close those Instruments and Engines knit,
> Which Motion, and their slender Sense transmit!
> Like living Watches, each of these conceals
> A thousand Springs of Life, and moving wheels.
> Each Ligature a Lab'rynth seems, each part
> All wonder is, all Workmanship and Art.

('Greatness in Little')[69]

Throughout the century, georgic and religious poetry reflected a similar awe at the miniaturized structure of creation. And, in response to the new standard of craft microscopically observed nature had set, poets often replicated patterns within patterns, as if simulating the wheels within wheels of the cosmic *machina*. For the discoveries of natural science not only suggested new complexities in nature, but raised questions as to where meaning resided. Was it hidden in inner structures, like an allegorical kernel; or was it an aura enveloping nature, whose interpretation 'brought it out only as a glow brings out a haze'—the mode of signification that Joseph Conrad and Teilhard de Chardin in their different ways would later formulate?[70] The margin of *sensibilia* might be only a frame of meaning, or a Jacob's ladder to it. Not that these questions at once reached metaphysical formulation. Instead, there was generally an excited wonder: a religious *meraviglia* such as informed the Renaissance aesthetic of *movere*.[71]

---

[69] Leigh (1947: 22–3).   [70] Conrad, *Heart of Darkness*, sect. 1 (1946: 48).
[71] Cf. Barolsky (1991).

The enhanced sense of complexity found correlates in literature's ubiquitous inset forms; in aedicules and other replicative features of architecture; and in the elaborate framing devices (often containing subsidiary images in medallions and the like) which characterized late gothic, Renaissance, and mannerist visual art. Ambiguity about the location of meaning affected the word 'frame' itself: it could refer not only to bracketing or containing elements, but also to the organizing structure, the *ordo* itself—the 'frame of sense'; 'a heart of that fine frame'; 'the very mould and frame'; 'this goodly frame, the Earth'. Artists of neo-gothic mannerism— all students, as it were, of Erving Goffman—would sometimes play on the ambiguity of the bracket's exact locus, by extending pictures on to their frames.[72] Or they would add labels that interacted with the contents; there is evidence of an Ovidian epigraph on the frame of Jan van Eyck's *Arnolfini* portrait—which itself frames an inset mirror image.[73] *Emblema* could mean insert; and the so-called emblem craze can be seen as a vast enterprise of assigning *inscriptiones* to images from nature or antiquity.

For literature, too, abounded with insets: complex Chinese boxes of narrative interlace, or miniaturized mythological insets like those in *Hero and Leander*:

> Her wide sleeves greene, and bordered with a grove,
> Where Venus in her naked glory strove
> To please the carelesse and disdainfull eies
> Of proud Adonis that before her lies.   (i. 11–14)

By such framing Marlowe assimilates the ancient gods into his modern discourse in a discriminating rather than merely syncretic way. Hero's sleeve has the fatal myth of Venus and Adonis inset in its border; while her myrtle wreath interweaves by allusion another myth, of Venus' defence of modesty. In drama, framing effects were more conspicuous still.

---

[72] Not a new device, however, as Christopher Braider claims: see Broderick (1982) for examples in Anglo-Saxon illumination.

[73] I am indebted to Paul Barolsky for this point.

Thomas Kyd's *The Spanish Tragedy* (acted 1592), for example, is thickly inset with masques-within-the-play. And the action of the main plot, which contains the masques, itself takes place within an allegorical framing action, in which Revenge and the dead Andrea perpetually keep watch from an upper stage on events below. This arrangement should not be seen as marginalizing the spiritual world. On the contrary, although the play is naturalistic by comparison with medieval Moralities, Kyd strongly asserts the comprehensiveness of divine judgement; plainly treating earthly life as a mission of reparation. More complex relations of frames and insets are to be found in Shakespeare. He was quick to see that, since *totus mundus agit histrionem* ('all the world's a stage'), the framing relation could be inverted or relativized.[74] Thus, Hamlet tests Claudius by insetting an interpolation in the already inset *Tragedy of Gonzaga*. At the performance within the performance, Hamlet and Horatio watch the King watching the player King in the Mousetrap, just as the audience watch all of them. But it is in the player's inset recitation, about Pyrrhus' excessive revenge, that the gods watching all of us make their compassionate appearance—'if the gods themselves did see' Hecuba, her cry 'would have made milch [milk-giving; moist] the burning eyes of heaven'[75]—with the result, perhaps, of chastening our ardour in identifying with Hamlet. The religious word was not always on the lips of the Reformer, in Renaissance drama. Instead, religion might be vestigial, or displaced on to surrogates, or implicit in symbolisms, or assimilated to feelings as natural as 'the gentle rain from heaven'.[76] Conversely, religion might transmute the natural; as when in *The Comedy of Errors* an enclosing frame of medieval divine comedy or romance serves to deepen the Plautine action.[77]

Only occasionally, in all these insets of nature or pagan

---

[74] Many examples are discussed in Barton (1967); see also Sutherland (1983); Fowler (1987). Among other dramatists, Robert Greene's framing is discussed in Braunmuller (1973).   [75] *Hamlet*, II. ii. 512–17; cf. IV. v. 202.
[76] Itself a biblical image: see Isaiah 55.   [77] Cox (1989: 64).

antiquity, do methodological implications become explicit. But insetting was ubiquitous; extending even to theoretical science. Something like Chinese boxes are clearly meant, when Margaret Cavendish writes 'Of Many Worlds in This World':

> Just like unto a nest of boxes round,
> Degrees of sizes within each box are found,
> So in this world may many worlds more be,
> Thinner, and less, and less still by degree:
> Although they are not subject to our sense,
> A world may be no bigger than twopence.[78]

The whimsical tone should not deceive one as to the sustained seriousness of her programme of poeticizing atomic theory.

The Unbroken Frame

What generally calls for examination, in framing effects, is how they change over a period of time.[79] Changes in the way medieval religious images were framed brought complicated, mixed consequences: the usual description ('secularization', 'rupture', 'breaking the frame') are less than adequate. For example, Simon Schama remarks how

In one of the most telling inversions of icons and objects in all of European religious art, the Dutch abolished images of the Madonna and Child from their churches, only to reinstate them surreptitiously as simple nursing mothers in paintings of church interiors. In many examples of the genre by Emmanuel de Witte and Gerard Houck-geest, Mariolatry has collapsed into mother-love. When nursing scenes are purely domestic, as in the great series by Pieter de Hooch, it should not surprise us to find them often placed immediately below sacred images.[80]

Although 'collapsed into mother-love' needs reformulation, Schama here convincingly draws attention to a characteristic

---

[78] Fowler (1991: 632).   [79] Goffman (1974: 54).
[80] Schama (1987: 540).

instance of reframing. Far from 'desacralizing', its effect was to reaffirm the potential sanctity of the domestic sphere and of individual human love. In another direction, an enhanced sense of creatureliness can similarly be discerned in enlargements of private individualism: Montaigne's never atheistic speculations; Shakespeare's meditative soliloquies; indeed, mannerist literature generally, with its self-reference and intense consciousness of the authorial self as *alter deus*.

All this intensified consciousness compensated, in Britain, for the half-century of reforming activism that followed rejection of the contemplative life. The monastic *vita contemplativa*, abjured at the dissolution of the monastic houses in 1536, began to return in multifarious new guises or variations— Ignatian spiritual exercises; metaphysical speculations; prolonged cogitations about emblems and *symbola*; and meditations on nature by writers as different as Robert Southwell and Henry Hawkins, Henry Vaughan and Anne Bradstreet.[81] One can almost speak of introspection as being widely cultivated throughout the intellectual community. This change was not always emotionally beneficial. Just as the emblem was a linear, rational form by comparison with manuscript illumination, so the new introspection could lack colour and nuance—could, indeed, become methodical, exacting, or repressive. At first, emblems and *symbola* like Alciato's and Bocchi's had been conceived as bringing together the deepest truths of Christianity; while Renaissance reconstructions of pagan mythology not only recovered ancient wisdom, but offered a sort of hermeneutic psychoanalysis.[82] But soon there was a cessation of the oracles. Reformers and Counter-Reformers alike repudiated such elusive activities. 'Right reason' was replaced by a narrower rationalism. And, within a century, Ficino's gentle syntheses and Bocchi's cautious accommodations had given way to sceptical anthropology or (more often) to crude attacks on paganism by such as Theophilus Gale (1628–78), of *The Court of the Gentiles* (1669–

---

[81] On the emblem fashion as a compensating movement, see Gilman (1986); Collins (1989: 21). [82] Watson (1993: 106).

77). The nine men's morrises and old cosmic mazes, the ceremonies of pilgrimage and purgation, were starkly proscribed as 'labyrinths of sin'.[83]

Systematizing, regularizing, and methodizing went forward in all spheres of life, not least in attitudes to the cosmos.[84] Nature, already a *fictio* in medieval allegory, was now internalized further, in the service of methodically subjective philosophies—of what Richard Baxter called 'Man's subjective religion'.[85] The importance Puritans attached to the duty of self-examination implied by 2 Cor. 13:5 ('Examine yourselves, whether ye be in the faith; prove your own selves') is well known. But self-consciousness also recognized itself in Descartes's epistemological observer: solitary, rational, introspective. In visual art, meanwhile, and later in literature, a geometrically coherent space-time was very gradually emerging. Eventually this was to make possible 'realistic' representations of the illusion of action continuously observed from a single spectatorial viewpoint. And in the political sphere, similarly, centralization promoted absolutism, whether pursued with machiavellian 'policy' or machine-like force—Spenser's iron Talus or heel of government. Everywhere, moreover, a minuter consciousness of time increased efficiency while decreasing contentment.

Among the discontents of self-consciousness seems to have been an intensified fear of death. Self-awareness, especially when combined with mortalism, scepticism, or lack of scepticism, easily brought a terror of mortality like Thomas Flatman's:

> When on my sick bed I languish,
> Full of sorrow, full of anguish,
>   Fainting, gasping, trembling, crying,
>   Panting, groaning, speechless, dying
>
>   .   .   .   .
>
> What shall I think, when cruel death appears,
> That may extenuate [lessen] my fears?[86]

('A Thought of Death', lines 1–4, 10–11)

[83] Cf. R. Hughes (1980: 395).   [84] Grant (1985).
[85] Baxter (1985, p. xxii).   [86] Saintsbury (1905: iii. 317).

Such apprehension is certainly different from medieval fears of judgement. Yet it may have as much to do with altered social relations and conceptions of nature as with decline of religion. To individuals at the centres of their several world-pictures, death could seem a black border, a terribly annihilating edge.

The new consciousness has been linked, and rightly linked, with the post-Copernican astronomical hypotheses that moved the old world's physical centre. The links, however, are not simple ones. Much excellent work in the history of ideas—notably two influential studies, Marjorie Nicolson's *The Breaking of the Circle* (1950, 1960, 1985) and Alexandre Koyré's *From the Closed World to the Infinite Universe* (1958)—has established how decisive the new discoveries were, in enlarging ideas of the physical world inherited from the Middle Ages, and in altering the very metaphors through which the world was perceived. But many of their readers seem to have formed the false impression that the old world's frame was simply exploded by expanding knowledge. No such annihilation took place; for reasons that will be explored in the chapters that follow. Late medieval and Renaissance thought was more dialectical than positivistic historians supposed, more used to entertaining discrepant cosmic models as speculative possibilities.

In art and literature of the period, similarly, one finds everywhere a vogue for disjunctive metaphors, paired or contrasted images, and complete pendant works: Donne's 'The Storm' and 'The Calm'; William Strode's 'Melancholy' and an answering 'Opposite to Melancholy'; Milton's *L'Allegro* and *Il Penseroso*; or, in visual art, Titian's *Sacred and Profane Love*; Rubens's *Het Steen* and *The Rainbow*; and even, at Urbino, Federico's Chapel and Studiolo, with its pagan Worthies.[87] Such couples need not be regarded as unresolved contradictions: sometimes they may have been felt as complementary contents, or opposite principles to be harmonized

[87] Vergara (1982: 118*a*).

into a deeper unity. And, in the same way, I believe, frames and central elements could complement one another. 'E.K.' seems to think along these lines in his Epistle before *The Shepheardes Calender* (1579):

in most exquisite pictures they use to blaze and portraict not onely the daintie lineaments of beautye, but also rounde about it to shadow the rude thickets and craggy clifts, that by the basenesse of such parts, more excellency may accrew to the principall; for oftimes we fynde ourselves, I knowe not how, singularly delighted with the shewe of such natural rudenesse, and take great pleasure in that disorderly order.

And Montaigne, too, in his essay 'Of Friendship', compares his own work to a painter's framing art: 'all void place about it [the picture] he filleth up with antike Boscage or Crotesko [grotesque] work; which are fantasticall pictures, having no grace, but in the variety and strangenesse of them'.[88] Starting from his source or model (in this case Étienne de La Boëtie's *On Willing Slavery*), the essayist adds a border around it: 'what are these my compositions in truth, other than antike workes, and monstrous bodies, patched and hudled up together of divers members, without any certaine or well ordered figure, having neither order, dependencie, or proportion, but casuall and framed by chance?' And the model of such Renaissance grotesque work was ancient: the antique ('antike') murals excavated in Rome.

So it was with the new frames devised by Renaissance intellectuals—*politique* statesmen such as Francis Bacon and poets such as Spenser and Donne; the Church Fathers and Councils and the doctrines of Augustinian theology still provided living ideas and decisive authorities.[89] Christian piety and pagan wisdom; religion and the secular; ancient and modern: these were not so much irreconcilable opposites as couples that interacted towards a long-term resolution. (Similar interactions have been traced between chivalric and

---

[88] Montaigne (1910: i. 195); see Colie (1973: 88).
[89] Cf. Hulse (1988); J. Martin (1992).

Christian values in the Middle Ages,[90] and between worldly and other-worldly ideals in Western architectural thought.[91]) Gradually, each contrary assimilated something of its 'opposite'. Classical example was valued for its antiquity, and hence its vestiges of prelapsarian nature; Christian art, for classical decorum and decency; the best of paganism, for its integrity and high standards. Imitation of classical antiquity, however, by no means dominated the transformation.[92] The very term 'secular' ('of this age') warns against this false simplification. Response to divine imperatives must be immediate; which, then, was more devout: doctrinal reformation or practical reform? Again, Renaissance culture may seem modern *vis-à-vis* medieval; but in the seventeenth-century *Querelle*, it often found itself on the side of the ancients. Meanwhile, although proponents of classical culture had promoted the new science in the sixteenth century, their eighteenth-century successors were firmly opposed to it.

If the imagination of the northern Renaissance was not secularized, the question arises when desacralizing began? The secularizing of politics, which used to be put very early, has been deferred by recent historiography.[93] Certainly all notions of a sustained 'progress' from religion to rationality at the Renaissance have been abandoned. Enthusiasm and superstition repeatedly fluctuated; as, for example, in the European witch craze, which persisted from the fifteenth century to the eighteenth while Christendom was threatened by Islam, ameliorating during the English Reformation but flaring again in the seventeenth century when central authority was weakened by doctrinal divisions.[94]

Closer to our subject are questions about how the rise of modern science affected 'traditional belief'. Some think it remained as a vestigial, ceremonial shadow of itself; others

---

[90] Curtius (1953); Keen (1984).   [91] Onians (1988, e.g. 130–5, 230–3).
[92] Cf. Onians (1988: 136).
[93] Contrast Christopher Hill and Stephen Collins with the revisionist and post-revisionist historians reviewed in Clark (1986, e.g. 166).
[94] Trevor-Roper (1969, ch. 3); Bossy (1985); Thomas (1988).

that it was repressed, like Matthew Arnold's 'buried stream'—
another displaced Freudian fluid. And what of religion's great
theme of resurrection? In approaching these topics my
method will not be philosophical or theological. I shall discuss metaphorics rather than metaphysics; hoping to track
changes in the religious imagination of the northern Renaissance, as these found reflection in tropes like framing, con-
struction, and stellification. This is not to assume, with the
young Huizinga, that visual images are best evidence (we shall
be concerned rather more with literature than visual art). But
one may suppose the imagination of the past to be more
accessible through its implicit, indirect expressions than
through explicit, official formulations.

Architectural Frames

Verrocchio's Edinburgh *Adoration all' Antico Madonna and Child*
shows the ruins of the Temple of Peace in Rome (identified
with the Basilica of Constantine), after its supposed collapse
into ruins on the night of Christ's birth. This was also the
night, according to legend, when the pagan oracles fell silent:

> The oracles are dumb,
> No voice or hideous hum
>   Runs through the archèd roof in words deceiving.

(John Milton, 'On the Morning of Christ's Nativity', lines 173–5)

Yet poets and artists of the Renaissance and the Reformation
not only treated pagan myths as oracular—profound, ther-
apeutic, salvific—but actually reconstructed the ancient
shrines earlier symbolically ruined. Pagan temple façades
were imitated in countless Christian churches by Brunel-
leschi, Bramante, Alberti, and Palladio, in a type so influential we take it for granted. I do not mention this extraordinary
fact with any idea of reviving that chimera of the nineteenth
century, recrudescent paganism. What we need to notice,
instead, is the extent of assimilation of ancient, renewed,

and recent religious themes. Pagan myths and ceremonial forms had become the metaphors of a Christian poetic religion. Self-sacrifice might be neglected by a corrupt Church, and liturgical sacrifice suspected by Reformers preoccupied with doctrinal correctness; but artists remembered and represented it vividly. Not only did they picture ancient sacrifice directly and in types symbolic of repentant self-sacrifice, like the flaying of Marsyas; they also alluded to sacrifice ubiquitously in architecture. As if to compensate for the emotional impoverishment of abolishing the medieval sacrificial mass, the religious motifs of classical ornament everywhere hinted at rites of immolation. Fillets round columns, Doric *bucrania*, altarlike forms, the numerical proportions based on the hecatomb: all spoke a language of sacrifice to those who knew their meaning—and unconsciously, perhaps, to many who did not.[95]

A cautiously outspoken chapter of Alberti's *On the Art of Building* discusses the 'sacrificial altar' and its siting. Putting the view for reform, he vehemently advocates a single altar: 'within the mortal world there is nothing to be found, or even imagined, that is more noble or holy than the sacrifice. I would not consider anyone who wanted to devalue such great things, by making them too readily available, a person of good sense.'[96] In his architectural theorizing, Alberti found nothing problematic about incorporating pagan forms; and others, like Antonio da Correggio, were ready to go astonishingly far in practice along the same line. The nave friezes in S. Giovanni Evangelista in Parma, from Correggio's cartoons, actually depict in detail ceremonies of pagan and of Hebrew sacrifice.[97] In Reformed churches, indeed, the tables of memorial communion pointedly replaced the altars of the sacrificial mass. Yet in so devout and so Protestant a poem as George Herbert's 'The Altar', where the sacrifice meditated

[95] Alberti (1988: VII. ix. 213) notices the calves' skulls and other 'sacrificial items' in Doric. Cf. Hersey (1988: 19 and *passim*); Onians (1988: 10) on hecatomb symbolism. [96] Alberti (1988: VII. xiii. 229).

[97] On attitudes implied by such syntheses, see Saxl (1939).

is as internalized as that of a contrite heart, nevertheless the shape of a sacrificial altar visibly appears. True, Herbert subtly transforms the pagan altar to a Christian column-altar. But not all his contemporaries, in their altar poems, even did that.[98] Robert Herrick, in 'The Sacrifice, by Way of Discourse betwixt Himself and Julia' goes so far (albeit with erotic intent) as to work through the entire procedure of an antique-cum-Hebrew ceremony—garlands, nard, wine, and 'trespass-offering'. Elsewhere, too, he freely introduces other features of ancient ceremonial, such as Lares and Penates. In 1648 these imagined revivals of Roman religion may have covered a longing for the almost equally ancient Christian ceremonies proscribed under the Commonwealth. Or perhaps the wish was for a ceremonial order that would be neither Laudian nor Puritan, neither papist nor Protestant.[99]

In the seventeenth-century estate poems, poems of welcome, and thanksgivings, sacrificial imagery was particularly common. Thomas Carew's 'To the King at His Entrance into Saxham, By Master Io. Crofts' sanctifies the ceremony of hospitality by asserting

> Instead of sacrifice, each breast
> Is like a flaming altar, dressed
> With zealous fires, which from pure hearts
> Love mixed with loyalty imparts.   (lines 5–8)

In Carew, the theme of sacrifice is unusually overt, as Rufus Blanshard and John Kerrigan have observed. But sacrificial implications integrated with classical imagery and diction are only less obvious in other poets. In Herrick's 'A Panegyric to Sir Lewis Pemberton', for example, the eucharistic elements of the common meal appear in the guise of Juvenalian satire. And Carew's estate poem 'To Saxham' follows Jonson, Martial, and Juvenal in imagining animals offering themselves, *sponte sua*, each as a willing sacrifice to the lord's table:[100]

---

[98] Westerweel (1983); Fowler (1995).   [99] Chambers (1992).
[100] 'To Saxham', lines 25–6 ('Every beast did thither bring | Himself, to be an offering'): Carew (1957: 28); cf. 'A New-Year's Sacrifice. To Lucinda' (1957: 32). On Carew's sacrificial and eucharistic imagery, see J. Kerrigan (1988).

The willing ox, of himself came
Home to the slaughter, with the lamb;
And every beast did thither bring
Himself, to be an offering.
The scaly herd more pleasure took,
Bathed in thy dish, than in the brook . . .   (lines 23–8)

Before long such vestiges of sacrificial thought were over-laid by further transforming strata. C. G. Jung relates a dream of descent through storeys of a personal building, down to ancient Roman and primitive levels; and our public architecture, similarly, has stories to tell of degeneracy and civilization. In John Wood I's Circus at Bath (1754), for example, the sacrificial symbols of the Doric order were replaced by symbols of crafts and professions. It was now professional life, apparently, that seemed to be sanctified, and that challenged devotion.[101] Later still, it was 'that great altar' of domestic life, as Dickens calls it, on which 'the best have offered up such sacrifices . . . as, chronicled, would put the proudest temples of old Time . . . to the blush'.[102] In our own century, many have discerned traces of the gothic cathedral in factories oriented by assembly-lines, or in supermarket aisles with their affordable eucharists. Or Sunday car-cleaning rituals may be inadequate transformations of ceremonies of purification. It seems even atheists cannot choose to have no religion; which makes it matter all the more that certain sorts of religion should be universally avoided.

In the course of the Renaissance the idea of the divine universe, far from dwindling, became strengthened, and its structures were established on a securer basis. Much early science, in fact, may be thought of as realizing religious aims. With this in mind, we shall explore certain forgotten

[101] On Wood's design, see Summerson (1963, ch. 4). On the sacrificial meaning of *bucrania*, see Serlio (1964: 140). The transition to the symbols of Wood's professional frieze had already began in the Renaissance, e.g. in Colonna's and Valeriano's interpretations of *bucrania* as labour: see Watson (1993: 136).   [102] *Barnaby Rudge*, ch. 81: Dickens (1986: 725).

aspirations of the Renaissance, in which sacred and worldly, scientific and religious mingled strangely. I shall focus on astronomy, the innovations in which made a great impact. Stellar imagery is so widely distributed in the literature of the period as to invite attention. Religion and science, rightly understood, never conflicted. But there was something of a *translatio imperii* from priests of ceremony to high priests of experiment. From time to time, ultimate objectives need to be reformulated. When Renaissance writers hoped for stellification[103]—as when they announced the Golden Age restored or claimed to raise the dead—their statements were not within the immediate sphere of science. Yet their aims, however distant, are of a sort that are still necessary, if the power of science is to be adequately oriented.

[103] Thomas (1988: 247). For literary examples of raising the dead, see e.g. Shakespeare, *Cymbeline, Winter's Tale*.

I

Histories of Heaven

When Elizabeth Drury died in December 1610, at the age of 14, John Donne, an acquaintance of the family, responded with the series of elegiac meditations known as *The Anniversaries*. In one of these neo-gothic 'twelve-month-minds' he laments that

> new philosophy calls all in doubt,
> The element of fire is quite put out;
> The sun is lost, and th' earth, and no man's wit
> Can well direct him where to look for it.

('An Anatomy of the World: The First Anniversary', lines 205–8)[1]

Donne may have meant this as *contemptus mundi* in the pessimistic spirit of Joseph Hall, another poet in the Drury circle. Or it may reflect popular bewilderment at the flood of new science or 'natural philosophy'—the ever more numerous discoveries, hypotheses, theories, and sceptical inferences by such writers as Henry Cornelius Agrippa (1486 Cologne–Grenoble 1535–6), urging the uncertainty of human learning. But the passage is far from implying that Donne thinks of science as an enemy to religious faith. To suppose that would be to confuse faith with certainty. Science, belonging to a different category from religion, could hardly 'challenge' it, as positivistic historians used to argue.[2] Often Renaissance

---

[1] On the circumstances of composition, see Manley (1963: 3 ff.); on Protestant precedents, Lewalski (1973).

[2] For the older view, see R. S. Westfall (1973). On scientism in the 17th century, see Southgate (1990).

science assisted belief by offering a *tertium quid* between high and low, abstract doctrines and material appearances.[3] Often, too, theological doctrines operated as a creative stimulus in the scientific sphere: Fr. Marin Mersenne of the order of Minims (1588–1648) was not the only scientist or 'Christian philosopher' who made discoveries by pursuing Augustinian ideas of universal harmony.[4] Renaissance science and theology interacted rather than diverged, in a period of fruitful dialogue. As Douglas Bush has remarked, no seventeenth-century belief was overthrown by science.[5] Yet it is just such 'evidence' that was tendentiously used to fuel acrimonious scholarly debate. Did sceptical rationalism triumph in the new science over theological obscurantism? Or was reform achieved in the teeth of scholastic rationalism, by Protestant theologians applying patristic ideas?

Theology and Science

In 1896 Andrew Dickson White could call his survey of the dispute *A History of the Warfare of Science with Theology in Christendom.* But serious scholars would now agree that the myth informing White's title obfuscates the true course of events. Renaissance science emerged from medieval science. It was fostered and formed as much as hindered by theology.[6] In the seventeenth century, moreover, the chief movers of the scientific 'revolution' were often prominent ecclesiastic figures. They are found indifferently on either side of the cultural partition that was to be invented, or at least exaggerated, in the nineteenth century. The astronomers John Wilkins and Seth Ward were bishops. Sir Thomas Browne, the author of *Pseudodoxia Epidemica* (1646), that most sceptical

---

[3] Funkenstein (1986); Rumrich (1987: 72–3).   [4] Dear (1990).
[5] Bush (1961: 50).
[6] Dear (1990); Mebane (1989); Henry and Hutton (1990); Brooke (1991); Maiorino (1990); and esp. Funkenstein (1986).

review of popular errors, was also capable of the enthusiasm for divine craftsmanship that eloquently informs *The Garden of Cyrus* (1658). Browne has turned out to be a better scientist than used to be thought. Sir Isaac Newton, however, now appears to have divided his time between discovering the laws we all remember and calculating the prophetic numerology we prefer to forget.[7] And William Oughtred told Aubrey he invented the slide-rule in order to calculate the date of the apocalypse. Religion, magic, and the new science were, indeed, increasingly distinguishable; but they were not yet disengaged. Religion sometimes lent authority to magic, sometimes reformed it away. Every science tells the same story, from the mathematical mechanics of Mersenne, whose brilliant research developed theological ideas of cosmic proportion, to the natural history of the Calvinist Constantijn Huygens or the physics and astronomy of Newton. But it is astronomy, queen of the Renaissance sciences, that invites closest attention.

Renaissance astronomy, with its combination of observational discoveries and extraordinarily wide-ranging, speculative hypotheses, was an important area of intellectual renewal. Change, however, was not rapid. Copernicus' heliocentric explanation of planetary motions brought no immediate revolution of ideas. It would be naïve to suppose that for anyone to deny after 1543 that the earth went round the sun must have been obscurantism like that mistakenly associated with Galileo's trial.[8] This is a *pseudoxion* of our time, so far undispelled by all Thomas Kuhn's and Hans Blumenberg's insistence on the comprehensive inclusiveness—and therefore inevitable slowness—of the Copernican revolution.[9] Copernicus' eventual victory was achieved only very gradually,

[7] Dear (1990) confutes Gellrich's idea that medieval totalizing contrasts with modern scepticism and piecemeal approaches.

[8] Shea (1972); Moss (1993). It is now thought that the trial had little to do with Galileo's planetary hypothesis.

[9] Kuhn (1985); Blumenberg (1987); for a critique of Kuhn, see Hoyningen-Huene (1993).

through a series of tiny incremental successes. Infiltration of the professional cadres of the astronomers; widespread adoption of the superior Prutenic Tables[10] (although Copernicus' system *qua* system was no more accurate); presentation of his ideas as mere hypotheses or paradoxes: all these, as Kuhn explains, slowly played out their parts.[11] His account of increments leading to 'paradigm change' nevertheless implies something a good deal tidier than the real creative chaos of Renaissance astronomy. A clear-cut choice between Copernican and Ptolemaic planetary systems was hardly ever in question. Instead, dozens of plausible, self-consistent hypotheses claimed attention, such as those of Tycho Brahe (1577: earth static, orbited by the sun, with heliocentric planets); Nicolaus Raimarus (1588: geocentric, with earth rotating); and Helisaeus Röslin (1597: earth static, with the outer planets orbiting both sun and earth).[12]

Ptolemy or Tycho?

The Jesuit polymath Fr. Athanasius Kircher (1602–80) was one of the best-informed thinkers of his time, passionate for knowledge; yet, even in 1656, when he surveyed the alternative planetary systems, he opted (as Donne probably did[13]) for the Tychonic hypothesis. This was not merely because Tycho's system disturbed the traditional world-picture less than Copernicus', but also for the good scientific reason that, being based on more accurate observations, it had better predictive value.[14] As for Blaise Pascal (1623–62), his rigorous standards of proof led him to express reservations about the Copernican system, no less than about Ptolemy's and Tycho's. He regarded the heliocentric hypothesis as a mere speculation

[10] Based on Copernican assumptions and published by Erasmus Reinhold in 1551. It was so named in compliment to Albert Duke of Prussia: patrons figured prominently in Renaissance astronomy.   [11] Kuhn (1985: 187–8).
[12] Riccioli (1651); Heninger (1977); Dreyer (1953); Taton and Wilson (1989).
[13] Bush (1961: 42).   [14] Merrill (1989: 26).

or *caprice*.[15] Contemporary lay opinion may be illustrated by William Hammond's verse 'You modern wits, who call this world a star [planet]':

> You modern wits, who call this world a star,
> Who say, the other planets too worlds are,
> And that the spots, that in the midst are found,
> Are to the people there islands and ground;
> And that the water, which surrounds the Earth,
> Reflects to each, and gives their shining birth;
> The brightness of these tears had you but seen
> Fall'n from her eyes, no argument had been,
> To contradict, that water here displays
> To them, as they to us, siderious rays.

> ('The Tears', lines 1–10)

This in 1655 differs little from Joshua Sylvester's casual mention of Copernicus' 'paradox', half a century earlier:

> And such are those (in my conceit at least)
> Those clerks that think (think how absurd a jest)
> That neither heav'ns nor stars do turn at all,
> Nor daunce about this great round earthly ball;
> But th' Earth itself, this massy globe of ours
> Turns round about once every twice-twelve hours:
> And we resemble land-bred novices
> New brought aboard to venture on the seas,
> Who, at first launching from the shoar, suppose
> The ships stands still, and that the ground it goes.

> (*Divine Weeks*, I. iv. 143–52)[16]

Kuhn dwells selectively on irrational opposition to Copernicus—on Protestant fundamentalist arguments and Catholic charges of heresy. Ecclesiastics certainly accused Copernicus (not without aptness) of rebuilding the Tower of Babel. But the objections reported by Du Bartas—for example, the destructive centrifugal force thought to be entailed by terres-

[15] Dijksterhuis (1986, ch. 4, sect. 270, p. 450).
[16] Saintsbury (1905: ii. 517); Du Bartas, I. iv. 143–52 (1979: i. 210). The idea is explicitly called a 'paradox', ibid. 178 (1979: i. 211).

trial rotation—were also made by the *politique* Jean Bodin. In the absence of gravity, the objections were hardly irrational. And the force of gravity, one should recall, had yet to be discovered.[17] The controversy about planetary systems was, in fact, a multi-faceted situation, and is not usefully construed as a contest between Copernican and anti-Copernican factions.

John Milton is supposed to have been too distressed by the Copernican revolution to get it into poetry. Yet if *Paradise Lost* VIII is read attentively, it will be found that the archangel Raphael there improvises a brilliant exposition of the planetary motions, putting the Ptolemaic, Tychonic, and Copernican hypotheses into proportion magisterially by making sense simultaneously in the terms of each:

> But this I urge
> Admitting motion in the heavens, to show
> Invalid that which thee to doubt it moved;
> Not that I so affirm, though so it seem
> To thee who hast thy dwelling here on Earth.
> God to remove his ways from human sense,
> Placed heaven from Earth so far, that earthly sight,
> If it presume, might err in things too high,
> And no advantage gain. What if the sun
> Be centre to the world, and other stars
> By his attractive virtue and their own
> Incited, dance about him various rounds?
> Their wandering course now high, now low, then hid,
> Progressive, retrograde, or standing still,
> In six thou seest, and what if seventh to these
> The planet Earth, so steadfast though she seem,
> Insensibly three different motions move?
> Which else to several spheres thou must ascribe . . .
>
> (*Paradise Lost*, VIII. 114–31)[18]

To the angelic mind, the choice between the various systems, it seems, is unimportant. Elsewhere, the poem develops at large the relativistic idea that the Ptolemaic system describes no

---

[17] Kuhn (1985: 191); Du Bartas, I. iv. 135–78 (1979: i. 210–11).
[18] See Kuhn (1985: 194–5), missing some of Milton's subtlety.

more than a corrupt contingency consequent on the Fall. Milton's sophisticated detachment from particular astronomical models seems to have been closer to Pascal's than Kuhn supposes. This is not to say that the possibility of forbidden knowledge never occurred to Milton.[19] But the topic of obscurantism in the early development of science needs no further emphasis at present.

In practice the Ptolemaic and Copernican systems seldom presented themselves as imaginative alternatives. In the Renaissance, mutually exclusive scientific models could coexist comfortably. Indeed, Ptolemy's model long survived as a well-tried option for astronomers: in 1651 Fr. Giambattista Riccioli still lists it among the serious contenders.[20] And even after the astronomers abandoned it, it continued to be useful to artists as the basis of countless iconographical programmes. In decorative art, it underlies virtually all baroque and rococo cosmic schemes. And do we ourselves not slip into Ptolemaic thinking when we speak of 'sunrise' rather than 'earthdrop'? (In much the same way, Copernicanism has lasted on into the Einsteinian world: we talk of the earth going round the sun, not describing a sinusoidal curve beside it.) In the seventeenth century, only a combination of Keplerian elliptical orbits, Newtonian gravity, and improved measurement settled—for a time—the planetary orbits. It ceased to be a matter of paradox and speculation, so that Sir Isaac Newton was able to say *Hypotheses non fingo*, 'I frame no hypotheses'.[21]

Abandonment of the Ptolemaic system was necessarily gradual, because astronomy had been the frame of almost all the old world-picture's multifarious interlocking components. Its complicated correspondences were connected through the planetary deities and zodiacal signs as if through a telephone exchange. Reordering the planets meant altering the entire intellectual world—metaphors, memory systems,

[19] See Schultz (1955).
[20] Riccioli (1651). Giambattista Riccioli, SJ (Ferrara, 1598–Bologna, 1671) at first opposed the Copernican theory, but later came to recognize it as the best hypothesis mathematically.   [21] *OED*, s.v. *hypothesis* 2.

encyclopaedias, and all. A change so comprehensive called for laborious preparatory phases, for example de-animation of the macrocosmic universe. Autonomous agency had to be eradicated from the astronomical world by a painfully slow, inchmeal process.[22] Johann Kepler (1571–1630) might calculate the orbits of the planets to be elliptical; yet, for many of his contemporaries, spiritual Intelligences haunted the ruins of the spheres. As we shall see, the stars were still often imagined in the late seventeenth century as consisting of soul-substance.

Meanwhile a similarly slow-paced process transformed the scale of the universe to make room for the astronomical phenomena hypothesized. During the Renaissance of monastic humanism the formidable Abbot Johannes Trithemius (1462–1516) already recommended geometry and arithmetic for their capacity to develop a sense of scale: 'By knowledge of the art of geometry you comprehend the dimensions of the world, which rise up out of numbers and measure.'[23] Cosmic scale is still hard to grasp; then, its enlargement must have called for great efforts. But one should not suppose the medieval universe to have been naïvely small. The ninth-century astronomer Al Fargani estimated the distance of the fixed stars as 75 million miles. And the *Image du monde* of 1245 (translated and printed by William Caxton in 1480 or 1481 as *The Mirrour of the World*), popularization as it was, put the distance at 65,357,500 miles.[24] In the Copernican universe of professional astronomers, it is true, the stars were seventy-five times as far away as in Al Fargani's Ptolemaic one. But in 1686 the best-seller *Entretiens sur la pluralité des mondes* by the popularizer Bernard de Fontenelle could still reckon 50 million leagues (125 million miles), only double Caxton's figure.[25] Such estimates of scale were not quickly revised.

[22] Dales (1980).   [23] Cit. Brann (1981: 290).

[24] Caxton (1913: 171); cf. Kuhn (1985: 81–2, 160). Koyré (1958: 34) wrongly supposes the medieval world to have been tiny.

[25] The best 17th-century estimates were of course a good deal larger. Burton's illustration is Tycho's estimate of the distance between Saturn's sphere and the firmament as 7 million semidiameters of earth: Burton, *Anatomy of Melancholy*, III. i. 2. ii (1989– : ii. 51).

Ideological Astronomy

Why did the 'new philosophy', with all its far-reaching implications, occasion so little distress? We have glimpsed one
reason in the slow pace of its introduction. Another may
have been its surprising acceptability to the ruling aristocra-
cies. Surprising, because the mythology of kingship depended
on astronomical space quite as much as on historical time.
The Ptolemaic position of Sol as the fourth of seven planetary
deities—centre, moderator, 'heart of the universe', *declarator
temporis*—had offered a powerfully validating cosmic image of
the medieval sovereign's status. Each was *primus inter pares*
among his nobles, so that Sol was often represented as a
ruler accompanied by six planet-counsellors.[26] Surely reordering the planetary system must subvert this natural validation of sovereignty? On the contrary. Heliocentrism made Sol
more powerful than ever, in fact; the sun was the universal
centre that earth and the other planets oribited round. Consequently, the Copernican hypothesis well suited the new style
of centralized monarchy. Louis XIV, absolutist sovereign *par
excellence*, was 'the Sun King'.[27] As if aspiring to stellar
apotheosis, he encouraged an elaborate solar cult whereby
his cosmic role was enacted in such ceremonies as the *levée*,
when as *declarator temporis* he rose to illuminate the courtiers
assembled in his bedroom at the exact centre of the Cour de
Marbre at Versailles. Facing his macrocosmic equivalent he
shone, from amidst the intricately symmetrical architecture,
directly eastward upon his country's capital. Louis was not
alone in his fondness for such symbolism. Throughout Europe, princes showed a keen interest in the new astronomy. On
his way to meet Anne of Denmark in 1590, for example, James
VI found time to visit Tycho at Hven. It is worth recalling,

[26] Fowler (1964: 73–4 n., 149, 189); Fowler (1970a, s.v. *numbers* 7); Du Bartas, 1.
iv. 551–64 (1979: i. 221–2).

[27] Mitford (1966); Macdonald (1984); Burke (1992); Berger (1993). On Copernicus' argument from the aesthetics and politics of the sun's centrality, see
Gingerich (1973: 97).

too, that planetariums and similar devices originated in palaces rather than universities.[28]

Because of this political dimension, and because astronomy was arousing great intellectual excitement, the skies soon became an arena of ideological contention. Powerful groups and individuals attempted to exert influence even among the stars. One important instance is calendar reform. With the help of a formidable team of astronomers and mathematicians (including Luigi Lilio Giraldi, Cristoph Clavius, and Egnatio Danti) Pope Gregory XIII carried through a reformation of the Julian calendar. Naturally this was resisted in Protestant countries: in Scotland until 1600, in Germany until 1700, in England, amazingly, until 1752. A less successful Counter-Reformation thrust was the attempt to Christianize the celestial globe. Two methods were applied. The first was to supply biblical equivalents like Bathsheba for Cassiopeia and Noah's Ark for Argo Navis (as in Wilhelm Schickard's *Atlas* of 1655). Alternatively (as in Julius Schiller's *Atlas Coelestis* of 1660), one could go in for arbitrary replacements—St Peter for Aries, St Andrew for Taurus, and so on through the twelve zodiacal signs.[29] Some Protestants took up similar ideas: the sombre wit Thomas Philipott advises:

> Next gaze on the Apostles, who do make
> (In heaven) a new and second Zodiac,
> For they were the twelve Signs, through which the Sun
> Of Righteousness his course on Earth did run.
>
> ('Considerations upon Eternity', lines 53–6)[30]

Perhaps Philipott remembered Donne's 'Litany'—'thy illustrious zodiac | Of twelve Apostles'. Thomas Carew also casts out the old constellations in *Coelum Britannicum* (1634), which owes something to Giordano Bruno's *Lo Spaccio della Bestia Trionfante*; although, as we shall see, Carew had more local,

---

[28] Zolla (1988: 64).   [29] G. S. Snyder (1984, pls. 49, 54, 55).
[30] Philipott (1950: 12).

Caroline replacements in mind. And George Chapman, following Gilles Durant, attempted erotic replacements:

> To open then the spring-time's golden gate,
> And flower my race with ardour temperate,
> I'll enter by thy head, and have for house
> In my first month, this heaven-Ram-curled tress:
> Of which, love all his charm-chains doth address:
> A Sign fit for a spring so beauteous.
>
> ('The Amorous Zodiac', lines 31–6)[31]

It is noteworthy that the reformed globes invariably retained many ingeniously accommodated mythological images, these having become indispensable in *artes memorativae* using the signs as places.

Historians persuaded by the so-called Merton thesis[32] contrast Catholic obscurantism in astronomy with Protestant progressivism; within seventeenth-century Protestantism, using a similar model, they see Puritans as more serious about science than their Arminian opponents. Such extreme *chiaroscuro* can no longer be regarded as convincing. In the Catholic countries, certainly, the establishment (including the universities) was often obscurantist; but there were also many adventurous scientists, both in academies and in religious orders.[33] It seems to have been the case that Calvinists in Holland and Britain more readily entertained the heliocentric hypothesis; so that Calvinism and Copernicanism were sometimes associated.[34] (This may have been because for Calvin the Bible was not a source of scientific information: conflict of authority need not arise.) But in any event the official Anglican doctrine of the Elizabethan Settlement was Calvinist; the

[31] Chapman (1962: 87–8). See Fowler (1970), App.; Smarr (1984: 380–1).
[32] A linking of the progress of science with the Protestant utilitarian ethic, which has come to seem simplistic: see Merton (1938), modified—insufficiently—in Kuhn (1977) and Cohen *et al.* (1990).
[33] Brockliss (1990) traces the slow adoption of Copernican astronomy in French universities. In Italy the process was slower still, caught up as it was in power struggles between the Jesuits and the Dominicans of the Holy Office.
[34] Hooykaas (1976); Bachrach (1962); Plumb (1969: 65 n.); Wittie (1681).

Royal Society was hardly Puritan; and many Puritans were more suspicious than serious about science.

The range and complexity of Renaissance attitudes to the stars may be emblemized by two tablets inserted in the façade of Laurieston Castle, Edinburgh. One is a late sixteenth-century astrological diagram, the 'celestial theme' or geniture of the son of the first owner, Sir Archibald Napier, father of the inventor of logarithms. The second tablet, put up by Robert Dalgleish, owner of Laurieston from 1656, seems to rebuke the first. Its inscription declares 'I do not acknowledge the stars as either the rulers of life or the causes of my good fortune. The things which I possess I ascribe to the goodness of God.' This is the inscription of a prominent churchman who served as solicitor to Charles I, the Protectorate, and Charles II in turn.[35] Dalgleish's wary sceptical fideism makes good sense, in view of the wildly excessive dependence on astrology and astronomy common in his time. Modern crazes for holograms, computer magic, or chaos-complexity theory offer only faint analogies with the excitement Renaissance astronomy aroused.

The fascination astronomy exerted was far more than a belief in astrology can explain. Nor is it quite enough to speak of the new appreciation of divine creativity that the new science prompted. The enthusiasm, which has never been adequately explained, will be explored in the next chapter. It is my belief that it had to do with discoveries imagined as blurring, or even breaking down, the immemorial division between mutable and immutable—between the corrupted and uncorrupted parts of the macrocosm. It seemed to many as if a route to immortality was opening up. For this reason more than any other, perhaps, the stars were fascinating. For one of the period's most prominent features is this obsessive fascination. Particularly after Tycho's discovery of the 1572 nova, stellar imagery appeared throughout Europe in every context, from heraldry to architecture, painting to poetry.

[35] Rowan (1974).

Stellar Imagery

A few typical examples may illustrate the ubiquity of the stellar obsession. So far as heraldry is concerned, William Camden notices many astronomical *imprese* in his *Remains*: one of Adam Newton's devices for Prince Henry was a hemisphere with stars.[36] House and inn signs might take the form of constellations, like the Seven Stars in Burchin Lane.[37] And there was a fashion around 1660 for 'comet glasses', wineglasses engraved with glittering comets.[38] Nor is the evidence by any means limited to such trivial indications. Some of the most celebrated art works of the period had astronomical programmes: one thinks of Michelangelo's twelve-pointed star in the Capitol pavement; of the velarium in Ottaviano Mascherino's Sala di Bologna; of the astrological cupola in the Pazzi Chapel at Santa Croce; and of the Sala dei Pontefici in the Vatican. There were several cosmic programmes within the Pitti Palace alone; and in the Boboli gardens the amphitheatre was redesigned in 1630–4 as a model of the zodiac, with niches corresponding to signs and hours.[39] The Star Chamber probably had a ceiling of stars, as the Sainte Chapelle had in Paris. Whole cities, such as the new Rome and Filarete's projected Sforzinda, were planned in the form of stars.[40] The cosmic design of Tycho's Castle of Uranienborg and the observatory of Stellenborg (1576) were other influential examples.[41]

Tycho spent the last two years of his life near Prague, where Rudolf II had a star-shaped hunting-lodge and park (Hvezda) built by his uncle Archduke Ferdinand of Tyrol. The garden in the form of concentric stars is described by Fynes Morison:

[36] Strong (1986: 145).   [37] Aubrey (1972: 273).

[38] Sutton (1992: 163–4).

[39] Fagiolo (1993). In 1661 a performance of *Mondo Festeggiante* gave theatrical expression to the same ideas. See also Seznec (1953: 76–82); M. Kemp (1992: 134).

[40] Manuel and Manuel (1979); Kostoff (1991: 15, 186 ff., fig. 183, index, s.v. *cosmic city, radial city*); Onians (1988, ch. 14); R. S. Westfall (1973).

[41] Heninger (1977: 166–8).

'The Emperor hath two enclosures walled about, which they call gardens, one of which is called Stella, because the trees are planted in the figure of stars, and a little fair house therein is likewise built, with six corners in form of a star.'[42] As Victor Skretkowicz has shown, Stella (which Sir Philip Sidney visited) was probably the model for Basilius' stellar lodge in the *Arcadia*, whose architecture Pyrocles wished to study: 'The lodge is of a yellow stone, built in the form of a star, having, round about, a garden framed into like points; and beyond the garden, ridings cut out, each answering the angles of the lodge.'[43] In the French style of landscape gardening, radiating avenues around the country house became a conventional feature, whether or not with a similar symbolism in view, of stellar rays. And one may speculate whether the radiating avenues of Paris, laid out at the same time as the gardens of Versailles, may have been intended to symbolize the power of the Sun King, as much as to exert it by allowing his artillery unobstructed fire. Astronomical gardens became fashionable, at least to the extent of star-shaped knots and concentric circles.[44] Sir John Wentworth's Somerleyton, with its musical automata and water garden, clearly evoked for Mildmay Fane a cosmic harmony:

> So have I observed,
> When walking near a stream, the heavens to be
> Beneath my feet, to ease Astronomy:
> There tell the Gamut of the Stars, and crack
> Of all their motions even with Tychobrack.

('To Sir John Wentworth', lines 100–4)[45]

Fane very often introduces such stellar imagery: it is for him, as for his friend Robert Herrick, a ready means of idealiza-

[42] *An Itinerary*: cit. Skretkowicz (1982: 177).
[43] Sidney, *New Arcadia* I (1987: 85–6, p. xxiv); see Skretkowicz (1982). Basilius' house was built in fact at Ampthill in England: see Aubrey (1972: 298) on Houghton Lodge.
[44] e.g. Lazzaro (1990: 41). In England, Twickenham Garden had a concentric plan. On cosmic diagrams in gardens, see Patterson (1981: 87).
[45] Fane (1879: 158); Fowler (1994: 229).

tion. Thus in 'A Buck-Hunting Journey to Belvoir' he imagines the members of a hunting-party and the circumstances of their entertainment as constellations, each appropriately assigned:

> There Lyra was to entertain
> The ears and feet of this bright train;
> And what Eridanus affords
> Was set with plenty on the boards.
> Thus shined they all that night; till morn
> Awaked the drowsy Capricorn,
> Who with the help of Aries' brow
> A 'hunt's up' to the rest did blow . . .   (lines 43–50)

In contemporary Dutch painting, the mere presence of a celestial globe was enough to indicate idealization;[46] and in the poetry, too, globes abounded.[47] Queen Elizabeth is portrayed as *regina universi* sustaining the spheres in a woodcut prefaced to John Case's *Sphaera Civitatis* (1588); and she used armillary spheres as a royal emblem, wearing them as earrings and embroidered on her sleeves.[48]

If Frances Yates is right, Shakespeare's Globe theatre, like Camillo's memory theatre, had twelve (or twenty-four) sides corresponding to the celestial signs, and a starry canopy (the heavens) above the stage.[49] In masques, whether at court or in private venues, stellar imagery was so frequent that Drummond of Hawthornden refers to the stars as 'Time's purpled masquers'.[50] Jonson's *Chloridia* is about a goddess 'to be stellified on Earth by an absolute decree from Jupiter, who would have the Earth to be adorned with stars, as well as the heaven'.[51] And the action and much of the imagery of Carew's *Coelum Britannicum* (1638) is similarly cosmic:

---

[46] Filipczak (1987: 186).   [47] Morgan (1983).

[48] Strong (1987: 139–40; figs. 144–50), showing armillary spheres on the attire of the Earl of Cumberland and Sir Henry Lee.

[49] Yates (1966: 355–9, 1969).

[50] Cf. Orrell (1985: 36–7) on the cosmic organization of *Vertumnus*, with characters representing the seasons, a twelve-branched tree, and a zodiac through which the sun moved, keeping pace with the play's action.

[51] Herford and Simpson (1925–52: vii. 750); see Strong (1979: 200).

Down from her azure concave thus I charm
The Lyrnean Hydra, the rough unlicked Bear,
The watchful Dragon, the storm-boding Whale,
The Centaur, the horned Goatfish Capricorn,
The Snake-haired Gorgon, and fierce Sagittar . . .   (lines 294–8)

'Neoplatonist' hardly seems an adequate description of such writing, it is so specifically astronomical. Carew almost inevitably symbolizes national reform as transformation of the heavens. Stage directions like 'danced in retrograde paces, expressing obliquity in motion' show the extent to which ideas were readily, at that date, imagined in astronomical terms.[52] The association of courtiers with particular constellations, however, calls for fuller exploration in a later chapter.

Literature of the Heavens

Although stellar idealization was common in all the arts, it pervaded poetry most of all. It was only to be expected that the Christian Muse should come to be identified as Urania, the ancient Muse of astronomy. Astronomical and cosmic poetry had had, indeed, an extensive history. There was enough of it to warrant inventing a special literary astronomy, a simplified system positing an ideal, changeless, primordial state of the heavens, untroubled by librations, precession, or stellar drift. The sixteenth-century efflorescence of astronomical literature, however, went far beyond anything previous. Only modern neglect obscures this. Before his death in 1960, Francis Johnson planned to follow his *Astronomical Thought in Renaissance England* with studies of the literary bearings of British astronomical writing.[53] These would doubtlessly have thrown light on the mysterious Renaissance passion for astronomy. Gabriel Harvey was aware of this enthusiasm. He notes that Leonard Digges has memorized the whole 'Aquarius' (book XI of Palingenio's

[52] Carew (1957, line 345).   [53] Johnson (1937, p. viii).

Zodiac of Life); Harvey himself, George Buchanan's *De Sphaera*; and Spenser, The Fourth Day of the First Week of Du Bartas's *Sepmaines*—some 1,000 lines describing the planetary system and 'the twinkling spangles of the Firmament'.[54] Spenser was ashamed of his lack of expertise with astronomical tables and instruments, though he knew something (Harvey has to admit) about the astrolabe and sphere.[55] Milton, later, was a friend of Galileo, and the culminating wish of Il Penseroso is for a hermitage 'Where I may sit and rightly spell | Of every star that heaven doth show'.[56] Christopher Harvey could even call church festivals 'quintessential extracts of stars'.[57]

It is usual to attribute much of this to Renaissance poetry's encomiastic function. And certainly astronomical imagery was indispensable in praising patrons to the skies. A striking example is Joshua Sylvester's translation of Du Bartas, with its interpolated panegyrics in italics. One of these interrupts the French poet's comparison of the sun's course with a royal progress to develop another analogy, with the tourneying course of Queen Elizabeth's Champion Sir Henry Lee:

> Day's glorious eye! even as a mighty king
> About his country stately progressing
> Is compassed round with dukes, earls, lords and knights
> (Orderly marshalled in their noble rites)
> Esquires and gentlemen, in courtly kind,
> And then his guard before him and behind.
> And there is nought in all his royal muster
> But to his greatness addeth grace and lustre:
> So, while about the world thou ridest aye,
> Which only lives by virtue of thy ray,
> Six heavenly princes, mounted evermore,
> Wait on thy coach, three behind, three before . . .

---

[54] Harvey (1913: 161); Du Bartas, i. iv, Arg. (1979: i. 206).
[55] Harvey (1913: 161–2): 'Pudet ipsum Spenserum, etsi Sphaerae, astrolabiique non plane ignarum; suae in astronomicis Canonibus, tabulis, instrumentisque imperitiae.'   [56] *Il Penseroso*, lines 170–1.
[57] 'Church Festivals': Fowler (1991: 348).

. . . .

> (As hardy Laelius, that great Garter Knight,
> Tilting in triumph of Eliza's right,
> (Yearly that day that her dear reign began)
> Most bravely mounted on proud Rabican,
> All in gilt armour, on his glist'ring mazor [helmet]
> A stately plume of orange mixed with azure,
> In gallant course, before ten thousand eyes,
> From all defendants bore the princely prize)
> Thou glorious champion, in thy heavenly race
> Runnest so swift we scarce conceive thy pace.
>
> (*Divine Weeks*, I. iv. 551–62, 599–608)[58]

A similar metaphor, it will be recalled, informs the framing allegory of *The Faerie Queene*, where each of the pageant heroes from Gloriana's court has 'like race to runne' (II. i. 32). Spenser's poem hardly suffers from his lack of mathematical astronomy, since its numerology is based on easily remembered astronomical constants. Redcrosse and Guyon accomplish their courses in just as many stanzas as correspond to the days and nights of solar and lunar years respectively.[59]

Panegyric serviceability, however, hardly begins to account for the abundance of astronomical poetry. The vogue is astonishing. Consider the case of the work Spenser memorized, Du Bartas's *Sepmaines*. A Latin translation appeared in 1591, while English versions, by Sylvester, William L'isle, Thomas Hudson, and others, came out piecemeal—thirty-three issues and new editions of the whole work or successive parts—by 1640. Even Simon Goulart de Senlis's commentary on the poem found translators (L'isle and Thomas Lodge). It is much the same story with Ovid, whose *Metamorphoses* were mostly stellification myths. He generated a crowd of translators, besides inspiring an entire school of English imitators—Marlowe, Shakespeare, Michael Drayton, and many lesser figures. At a more plebeian level, Christopher Middleton (who turned his hand to anything popular, from romances

---

[58] Du Bartas (1979: i. 221–3).   [59] Fowler (1964, chs. 8 and 9).

to the art of swimming) brought out *The History of Heaven: Containing the Poetical Fictions of All the Stars in the Firmament, Gathered from among All the Poets and Astronomers* (1596), based for the most part on Ovid's myths. And John Taylor the lowbrow Water Poet has a zodiac of epigram-sonnets, besides much spoof astrology. Astronomical poetry soon flourished in America, where Spenser was an early favourite. An anonymous colonial georgic of about 1651 develops a Spenserian calendar in zodiacal yet highly anthropomorphic terms:

> The crabfish climbs and posts along,
> The red cheeked Virgin (quite forlorn),
> The roaring rampant Lion strong,
> The sturdy well-set Capricorn.

> The Bowman's swift, the Serpent creeps,
> And Libra rumbles in the sky,
> The Waterman in Vulcan leaps,
> And Pisces spouts the flames on high.

['Resplendent Studs of Heaven's Frame', lines 49–56][60]

The specific descriptions here allow one to glimpse how immediately astronomical phenomena were once experienced.

Two important poems, Sir John Davies's *Orchestra* (1596), and Milton's *Comus* (1637), belong to a tradition, going back to Plato's *Timaeus*, of a *choresis*, or cosmic dance, of time's masquers, the planets and constellations.[61] The symbol of *choresis* underlies the programmes of many Renaissance masques and *ballets de cour*; politically understood, it implies a harmonious, 'natural' disposition of affairs. The plot of *Orchestra* turns on whether Queen Penelope will accept her suitor Antinous' invitation to join in a courtly dance not hard to recognize as 'the olde daunce' of love. Antinous' line is to disguise it in the higher strain of Thoinot Arbeau's *Orchésographie* (Langres, 1589) as the eurhythmics of nature's round.

[60] Meserole (1968: 507).
[61] *Timaeus* 40: see Miller (1985); Freccero (1968); Doob (1990: 285 and ch. 10 *passim*). Cf. Herbert, 'Vanity (I)' (1941: 5).

But faithful Penelope prefers the *choresis* of the celestial Venus to *la ronde* of Venus naturalis. If one expects that in this exchange the seducer will be the dangerous innovator, there is a surprise in store. It is Antinous who holds to the traditional Ptolemaic system, refusing 'to allow the Earth to dance to the new Copernican tune'.[62] Davies seems to associate moral reformation with reform of the planetary system.

Like Antinous, the festive Comus claims that he and his revellers are doing what comes naturally:

> We that are of purer fire
> Imitate the starry choir,
> Who in their nightly watchful spheres
> Lead in swift round the months and years.   (lines 111–14)

To some critics of this famous passage, Comus' dance is authorized by the *choresis* of the planets' 'starry choir'. The Attendant Spirit, however, speaks more responsibly of spiritual purification and the soul's marriage 'far above in spangled sheen' with a 'Celestial Cupid' (lines 1002–3). Which view is nearer to Milton's own? He himself answers this, in a striking way, by underwriting the Attendant Spirit's higher authority in the form of the poem. For the line-total of the entire masque is a number familiar in the Renaissance: 1,022, the total number of fixed stars in Ptolemy's star catalogue. Thus, the poem's proportions do not confirm Comus' appeal to the planets' 'watchful spheres' in their 'swift round'. Instead, the line-total—as it were, the poem's bottom line— insists on the slower, larger *coelum stellatum*, the sphere of the 'fixed' stars in their long precession.

How far could Milton expect such a device to be noticed? So far as his educated 'fit audience' was concerned, he had no problem: a knowledge of number symbolism in literature was widely shared by well-grounded readers.[63] But one may suspect that his numerological 'secrets' may have been open

---

[62] Manning (1985: 180).
[63] On Renaissance numerology, see Fowler (1964); I. C. Butler (1970); Fowler (1970a); Patrides (1982, ch. 4); MacQueen (1985); Røstvig (1994).

to a somewhat wider group. For the habit of counting verses was deeply engrained among all who could claim to be lettered, through the practice of memory-art. Star-totals of constellations would be familiar from applications such as visual art, pageantry, heraldry, and house signs; and for more systematic information there were many easy digests of Ptolemy's *Almagest*, like Piccolomini's *De le Stelle Fisse*, besides more popular treatments, like those of Palingenio and Middleton. Many incidental references in Renaissance literature argue familiarity; as when Sylvester mentions the 'three gold rings . . . With sixe gold strings' of the Balance,[64] or Drayton casually introduces the count of the extra-zodiacal constellation Perseus:

> And thou brave Perseus in the Northern air,
> Holding Medusa by the snaky hair,
> Jove's shower-begotten Son, whose valour tried,
> In seventeen glorious lights are stellified.
>
> (*Endymion and Phoebe* (1595), lines 365–8)[65]

It may be instructive to glance at the context of the last instance, in *Endymion and Phoebe*, Drayton's much-imitated Neoplatonic modulation of erotic Ovidian epyllion. The climax of Phoebe's wooing comes when

> She in a fiery mantle doth him wrap,
> And carries him up from this lumpish mould
> Into the skies. (lines 664–6)

Through 'the clearest element of fire', then, 'doth she mount him up into her Sphere, | Imparting heavenly secrets to him there'. Revealing the planetary motions, she ascends 'to lift him to the starry firmament'.[66] A subsequent encomium on the ennead notes that

---

[64] Du Bartas, I. iv. 253–4 (1979: i. 213).
[65] Drayton (1931–41: i. 138).
[66] Lines 679, 681–2, and 720. With the mantle, cf. Jonson, *Underwood*, LXXXIV. iii: 'And let there be a starry robe | Of constellations 'bout her hurled'; and the wrapping of the arras canopy or 'heavens' round Tamyra in Chapman's *Bussy D'Ambois*.

those rare men which learning highly prized
By whom the Constellations were devised,
And by their favours learning highly graced,
For Orpheus' harp nine stars in heaven placed . . .   (lines 943–6)

This is certainly didactic verse—an early instance, in fact, of English georgic. It does not read, however, like a cold lesson in abstract astronomy or Neoplatonic mathematics. Drayton's enthusiasm is undeniably engaged. Although his powers cannot always answer the inspiration, Phoebe has kindled him, like Endymion, 'with this celestial fire'. She resembles the maid crowned with stars in alchemic ascesis, who represents a divine knowledge raising the initiate to the stellar sphere.[67]

Drayton's cosmic journey is not altogether easy to place among the many others of the seventeenth century and earlier. Ancient literature treated space travel perfunctorily. In Lucian's *Verae Historiae* and Seneca's *Apocolocyntosis* it remains strictly subservient to the satiric purpose; and much the same is true of Phaeton's fatal journey in the *Metamorphoses*, however vividly Ovid animates the disturbed constellations. Macrobius' *In Somnium Scipionis*, a fundamental authority for the Middle Ages, offers a closer view of the spheres, and clearly remains a model for Drayton. But here, as in the elaborately allegorical medieval philosophical epics built on Macrobius and Martianus Capella—Bernardus Sylvestris, Alanus de Insulis, and the rest—the journey is an inner one: an ascent of reason from topic to topic of erudition or wisdom.[68] As with medieval philosophy itself, empirical observation did not play a principal role. The difference is striking when one comes to Dante's *Divina Commedia* and—still more—to Chaucer. With them, the astronomy, while still primarily serving as an ordering principle, is detailed enough for the journeys to call to a modern reader's mind thoughts of science fiction.

[67] See Abraham (1990: 224–5), citing Ripley. Drayton was sometimes chaffed about his number symbolism: see Drayton (1931–41: v. 22).
[68] Cf. Curtius (1953: 110).

This impression continues with Astolfo's journey to the moon in the *Orlando Furioso*, and intensifies when one turns to Satan's and Raphael's flights in *Paradise Lost*. Drayton's *Endymion and Phoebe* represents a transformation of the medieval genre, in that instruction about the external cosmos is more detailed, particularly where numbers of stars are concerned.

In this change, the pivotal poetic work is Spenser's *The Faerie Queene*. The ascent of Dame Mutabilitie into the spheres is no mere allegorizing of a realization already arrived at by astronomers: namely, that corruption extended (as, for example, in the solar *maculae*) further into the cosmos than had been supposed. For Spenser profoundly revalues this discovery, when he imagines Nature's enigmatic verdict as partly favourable to Mutabilitie. Far from being condemned, she is recognized as the historical process. Moreover, to decide the issue, reason now proceeds less by abstract ratiocination than by reviewing—in one of the finest passages of the poem—evidence from temporal change and patterns of change. Later, with the seventeenth-century fictional journeys of Cyrano de Bergerac and others,[69] and treatises such as those of Francis Godwin, John Wilkins, and Pierre Borel, attitudes became still more oriented to astronomical discoveries, and to possibilities of physical space travel. When one thinks of the baroque *coups d'œil* of Milton's spatial visions, the difference from Dante's inner journey seems immense. Milton may wish for inner, moral and spiritual, journeys; but his imagination delivers images of external, unmoralized astronomy, quite as detailed as Drayton's, and more spatially conceived.

In poetic astronomy as in Neoplatonism, Drayton learnt much from Spenser, whom he imitated freely. He candidly acknowledges this: he has presumed to 'sing by' his 'Deare Collin'.[70] Drayton if anyone would have appreciated what now seem astonishingly hermetic extremes of difficulty in *The Faerie Queene*. I have in mind the device whereby

[69] See Nicolson (1961).
[70] *Endymion and Phoebe*, lines 993–4: Drayton (1931–41: i. 155).

characters are grouped according to the stars in an appropriate constellation. In the Bower of Bliss, for example, a place of Venus naturalis, the eight characters match the eight stars of Libra, the constellation corresponding to the sign Libra, Venus' domicile.[71] Spenser's allegorical houses are in this way linked with astrological houses: a formal subtlety he very likely learned from Chaucer.[72] The device depended on—and in turn would foster—knowledge of poetic astronomy. Similar information was expected in readers of *Prothalamion*, whose unusual stanza of eighteen lines is determined by the star-total of Gemini, the 'twins of Jove . . . Which decke the Bauldricke of the Heavens bright'.[73] The poem is a bridal song for a double spousal; Spenser imagines the bridegrooms Henry Guilford and William Lord Petre as analogous to Castor and Pollux, types of faithful friendship. This conceit is worked out in the poem's imagery and narrative sequence; so that its very structure implies a fashioning of gentlemen into stellified, virtuous substance.

Spenser was not alone in writing in this way. Throughout Renaissance literature, an astronomy we have lost is closely woven into the texture of association, memory, and thought. Even in poems of strong, intimate feeling, it sometimes forms a vital connecting strand. A good example is Richard Lovelace's 'The Grasshopper', that bold defiance of the Commonwealth:

> Our sacred hearths shall burn eternally
> As vestal flames; the north wind, he
> Shall strike his frost-stretched wings, dissolve and fly
> This Aetna in epitome.
>
> Dropping December shall come weeping in,
> Bewail th' usurping of his reign;
> But when in show'rs of old Greek[74] we begin,
> Shall cry he hath his crown again!   (lines 25–32)

[71] Guyon, Palmer, Acrasia, Verdant, Genius, Excess, and two damsels: see Fowler (1964: 116). In poetic astronomy, constellations and corresponding signs were often in effect conflated.   [72] North (1988: 363–5; cf. 473).
[73] See Fowler (1964: 175; 1975, ch. 4).   [74] Both wine and language.

Modern readers have forgotten that these familiar lines trace the seasons of discontent in the skies as well as in the political arena. Royalist 'sacred hearths' are like 'Vestal flames' in large part through association with the vestal altar, Ara, a constellation in Scorpio. (The fire was not only one of hospitality and of zeal: mythologically, the altar was where the Olympian gods swore an oath of unity against the rebellious Giants.[75]) Scorpio is November's sign, while 'Dropping December . . . shall cry he hath his crown again' in the sense that Corona Meridionalis is in December's sign, Sagittarius.[76] Once, most readers would have known that the constellations Lovelace refers to were enacting the seasonal round. Few would have needed to consult a planisphere or celestial globe.

—Certainly not Mildmay Fane, who uses imagery not unlike Lovelace's in his 'Sapiens Dominabitur Astris':

> Poise Libra's Balance and bring on
> Allay to fiery Scorpion
> And Chiron's double shape betray
> When Saturn horsèd Philera,
> Bringing the lustful Goat to mind.
> When winter solstice proves unkind
> And for to drain Aquarius send
> For undertakers of the Fen,
> That Fishes may enjoy their ease
> In larger shape in boundless seas,
> And Cetus satiated thus
> Swallow and spout Eridanus.   (lines 37–48)[77]

Fane, like Lovelace, turns as spontaneously to stellar imagery as to that of terrestrial nature.

None of the astronomical literature of the Renaissance suggests that the scientific revolution occasioned overwhelming doubt or loss of faith. On the contrary, it suggests rather enthusiasm and excitement. Of course there was uncertainty

---

[75] See e.g. Piccolomini (1548, fo. 81ʳ).
[76] Other constellations alluded to at appropriate locations in the poem include Crater and Libra. Consult a celestial globe, planisphere, or star map (e.g. G. S. Snyder 1984: 63, 83).   [77] Fulbeck MS 'Poems 1655', fol. 84ᵛ.

about the many astronomical hypotheses of the day. Yet the discoveries of Copernicus and Galileo, Tycho and Kepler, seem to have had a surprisingly positive impact. For example, they seem to have had the cumulative effect of encouraging a revived Pythagoreanism. They excited stellar aspirations of a strange sort, whose specific nature we have next to explore.

2

Stellar Afterlives

In the Ducal Palace of Urbino, among the *trompe-l'œil* intarsias in the Studiolo of Federico da Montefeltro (1422–82), there is a fictive *cartellino* bearing the inscription VIRTUTIBUS ITUR AD ASTRA. It would be simplistic to take this to mean 'through virtues one scales the heights'. Federico the great military and political leader, magistrate, and city planner, who designed every minutest embellishment of his study, would hardly have enshrined in it such a cliché. The inscription more likely echoes Apollo's approval of Iulus' military heroism in the *Aeneid*: 'so man scales the stars', together with the conclusion of the *Purgatorio*, where the renovated (*rifetto*) Dante prepares *salire a le stelle.*[1] Federico aspires to Christian honour; he reads Virgil in the spirit of Constantine's famous inscription in St Peter's, MUNDUS SURREXIT AD ASTRA TRIUMPHANS, 'through Christ the world has risen triumphant to the stars'.[2]

More strangely stellar is the ascent Edmund Spenser desires, in the 1594 ode for his own marriage:

> And ye high heavens, the temple of the gods,
> In which a thousand torches flaming bright
> Doe burne, that to us wretched earthly clods
> In dreadful darknesse lend desirèd light;
> And all ye powers which in the same remayne,
> More then we men can fayne,
> Poure out your blessing on us plentiously,
> And happy influence upon us raine,
> That we may raise a large posterity,
> Which from the earth, which they may long possesse,
> With lasting happinesse,

[1] *Aeneid* 9. 638–44; see Cheles (1986: 63) and cf. Barolsky (1990: 132).
[2] Onians (1988: 59).

> Up to your haughty pallaces may mount,
> And for the guerdon of theyr glorious merit
> May heavenly tabernacles there inherit,
> Of blessèd Saints for to increase the count.
>
> *(Epithalamion,* lines 409–23)

There is nothing strange about praying for a large family at a time when birth-rates in Europe were only beginning to keep pace with deaths from disease and famine. One recalls the seventeen children Mrs Francis Quarles bore, or John Colet, sole survivor of twenty-two. But, even allowing for the conflation of angels with spiritual Intelligences guiding the spheres,[3] one wonders what the stars and their number have to do with the afterlife of Spenser's offspring. There are, indeed, relevant texts in the Bible, and rather more in the Apocrypha. God says to Abraham 'Look now toward heaven, and tell [count] the stars, if thou be able to number them . . . So shall thy seed be.'[4] In Psalm 147: 4 'He counteth the number of the stars, and calleth them by their names,' which, as John Donne notes, 'many expositors interpret of the elect'.[5] In Job 25: 5 'the stars are not pure in his sight'. In Daniel 12: 2–3: 'Many of those who sleep in the dust of the earth shall awake. . . . And those who are wise shall shine like the brightness of the firmament, and those who turn many to righteousness like the stars for ever and ever.' And especially in Matthew 13:43: 'Then shall the righteous shine forth as the sun in the kingdom of their Father,' with its implication of ressurection through the rising Sun of Righteousness.[6] As

---

[3] e.g. Donne, 'Air and Angels'; also Cowley, *Davideidos* 1. 76–7: 'Exultant homines, exultant agmina coeli | Sidera calcas . . . '.

[4] Gen. 15: 5; cf. 22: 17, 'I will multiply thy seed as the stars of heaven'; Neh. 9: 23; etc. Cruden's *Concordance* anachronistically demythologizes this: 'the number of the stars was looked upon as infinite: and the Psalmist, to exalt the . . . infinite knowledge of God, says, that he numbers the stars, and calls them by their names. . . . When the scripture would express a very extraordinary increase and multiplication, it uses the similitude of the stars of heaven.'

[5] *Essays in Divinity* (wr. 1614–15?): Donne (1952: 52).

[6] Cf. 1 Enoch 62: 13–16 and 104: 2, 4; 2 Baruch 51: 5, 10; 1 Cor. 15: 35–43; Matt. 22: 30–1; etc. On the Sun of Righteousness (Mal. 4: 1), a prominent symbol in Christian art of the time, see Panofsky (1955: 286–8).

biblical metaphor, canonical enough. But Spenser's 'haughty pallaces' seem more material, like Milton's 'argent fields' which 'Translated saints, or middle spirits hold | Betwixt the angelical and human kind'.[7] It is as if a stellar realm is meant, where the spiritual élite are to enjoy a renewed material life.

Such ideas are not only poetic fancies; they occur in sober prose. Among Izaak Walton's materials for a life of John Hales (1584–1656), the educator and fearless champion of the poor, is an introduction to Hales's sermons, drafted by Anthony Farindon the biographer (1598–1658). Hales, writes Farindon, now 'hearkens after no trumpet but the last':

> the souls of just men made perfect look not back neither on our imagery nor our worship, but shine as stars, which are not seen, but by that light which streams forth in the memory of those virtues which raised and fixed them there; but see no more of us, than those stars (to which they are likened) do, when we move and walk by their light.[8]

We are influenced by the light, guided by the example of the stellified dead. In extending the stellar analogy, Farindon does not present it as an *ad hoc* invention but as a familiar biblical comparison—'they are likened'. Jonquil Bevan is surely right to associate the passage with the intense contemporary speculation about what might be expected to intervene between death and judgement. This was the topic, for example, of Jeremy Taylor's funeral sermon for Sir George Dalston in September 1657—which, however, remains determinedly agnostic as to the whereabouts of the intercalary life.

To return to Farindon: if he means simply that Hales has gone to heaven, why say so much about stars? Doing so incurred needless theological risks. There was the danger, for example, of getting mixed up with stellar 'gods'—like

---

[7] *Paradise Lost*, III. 460–2. On 'translated saints' like Enoch (Gen. 5: 24), see Huttar (1964: 86–8).

[8] Bevan (1989: 167). Farindon, a noted Royalist preacher who suffered much during the Interregnum, was a cautious Latitudinarian.

'the bishop of Rome' in John Foxe's remark, who 'for his abominable pride is fallen from heaven' and thought 'to stellify again himself there whence he fell'.[9] Lucifer's starry host were after all Jehovah's enemies.

Hermetic and Pythagorean Ascents

The Spenserian passage quoted earlier compresses many ideas and scraps of world-picture. An aspiration to be stellified (translated to the stars) went back to antiquity, when general belief linked the soul's immortality with the heavens. Franz Cumont, once counted the learned psychopomp of the Roman afterworld, presented this belief as a syncretic conglomeration of ancient Greek star worship, notions of stellar soul-substance, and Eastern astrology.[10] More significantly for the present enquiry is the tradition of quasi-religious Pythagoreanism. Two main lines of subsequent development are distinguishable, the Pythagorean–Platonic and the Hermetic. According to Hermetic theory, the soul accomplishes a cosmic journey through gestation, life, and death. It descends through the spheres, receiving en route various planetary endowments, which are implanted in the embryo as potentialities or seeds of virtues. Then, during the seven ages of life, the soul reascends through the planetary spheres in reverse order, until at last, if it has achieved gnosis, after death it completes its journey in the unchanging stellar sphere.[11] In medieval realizations, the Hermetic doctrine was presented sketchily, with little by way of psychological detail. The soul in its journey was merely said to pass through the

[9] For this and similar usages see OED, s.v. stellify.
[10] Cumont (1922); Pauly and Wissowa (1893– : l. 141). See now Temporini and Haase (1972–).
[11] Porphyry, De Antro Nympharum (1991: 44–5, 61–5); Macrobius, In Somnium Scipionis, I. 12 (1952: 133–7); see M. J. B. Allen (1990). The Gnostic Ophites believed that Christ descended through the seven heavens at Jesus' baptism, and took away the seven Archons' powers: see Hermetica (1992: 116–17).

crystalline spheres. When Chaucer's Troilus dies, 'His flighte goost [spirit] ful blisfully is went | Up to the holughnesse of the eighthe spere', from which concavity he looks down 'with ful avysement' on the 'erratic sterres' below—the seven planetary spheres—and hears their 'hevenyssh melodie'.[12]

On the authority of late antique interpreters of Plato like Macrobius, the dead entered the stellar sphere through the sign of Capricorn. Consequently Cancer and Capricorn, the tropical signs limiting the sun's ecliptic path, were known as 'portals of the sun'. Cancer was 'the portal of men' because souls descended through it into terrestrial life, Capricorn 'the portal of gods'.[13] The idea survived in Renaissance textbooks like Valeriano's *Hieroglyphica* (1556). It may inform such funerary monuments as the Prince David monument in All Souls Conington (*c.*1613), designed by Sir Robert Cotton, which uses the ancient funerary chest motif of a triumphal arch or portal. The 'great gate of death', symbolizing entry to a celestial realm, is discussed in the anonymous paper (perhaps by Cotton himself) read to the Society of Antiquaries in 1600.[14]

Hermetic doctrine excited Renaissance intellectuals in the Paracelsian or anti-Aristotelian orbit. The soul's journey provided a theme for the Polish Horace, Casimir Sarbiewski (1595–1640), and in England for Henry Vaughan. Vaughan's 'The Importunate Fortune' lists the stages, combining them with a satiric testament:

> My growing faculties I send as soon
> Whence first I took them, to the humid Moon.
> All subtilties and every cunning art

[12] *Troilus and Criseyde*, 1808 ff. For interpretations of the passage, see North (1988: 29–32); I differ from North in taking 'holughnesse' (line 1809) to mean 'hollowness, concavity' and so to imply an *eighth* sphere.
[13] *In Somn. Scip.* 1.: Macrobius (1952: 133–7); see Fowler (1964: 71 and 99–100). The soul's immortality is discussed in *The Zodiac of Life* under *Capricorn*: Palingenio (1947: 198). For cosmic soul-journeys, see also Kepler (1634); Kircher (1656).
[14] D. Howarth (1992: 10); Hearne (1771: i. 235): 'The shape of a great gate or house intimateth, that the deceased are received into houses by the great gate of death, there perpetually to remain in happiness.'

To witty Mercury I do impart.
Those fond affections which made me a slave
To handsome faces, Venus thou shalt have

.   .   .   .

My ill-placed avarice (sure 'tis but small):
Jove, to thy flames I do bequeath it all.
And my false magic, which I did believe,
And mystic lies, to Saturn I do give.
My dark imaginations rest you there,
This is your grave and superstitious sphere.
Get up my disentangled soul, thy fire
Is now refined and nothing left to tire
Or clog thy wings. Now my auspicious flight
Hath brought me to the Empyrean light.
I am a sep'rate essence, and can see
The emanations of the deity,
And how they pass the seraphims, and run
Through every throne and domination.

(lines 59–64, 69–81)[15]

(Vaughan follows the Ptolemaic order of the planets, as does his source, the *Corpus Hermeticum*.[16]) Psychologized rendering of ancient ideas is characteristic of Vaughan's century; but he strikes an individual note of mystical simplification when he represents the ages of life as mere entanglements of his soul's essence.

The Pythagorean–Platonic line of ideas was no less strange. In Platonic doctrine, stars were conceived as living beings— not a specially farouche notion when all nature was alive. (Aristotle was later to teach his pupil Alexander the Great that 'heaven is full of the gods to whom we give the name of stars'.) Plato speaks of the Creator as having 'allotted souls equal in number to the stars, inserting each in each';[17] and he appears to have thought of the virtuous as returning after life on earth to their 'associate' stars, to spend a blessed existence.

---

[15] 'The Importunate Fortune': Vaughan (1957: 636). For Sarbiewski, see Røstvig (1954: 280–5).
[16] I. 24–26: *Hermetica* (1992: 6), replacing (1985: 126–9); see Vaughan (1957: 758). On Giordano Bruno's Hermetic version of Copernicanism, see Yates (1984: 260).   [17] R. H. Allen (1963: 26).

Stellification

The poets seemed to be more specific. True, the words of Ovid's Medea may be discounted as hyperbole, when she says her head will touch the stars (*vertice sidera tangam*). But many of the metamorphoses end in unambiguous stellification. Hercules, Castor and Pollux, the seven daughters of Atlas: all these and many more are translated to the stars. (Even Berenice's hair is put into orbit—a stellification, renowned in the seventeenth century,[18] that Alexander Pope will make use of in the conclusion of *The Rape of the Lock*.) Ovid risks a closer approach to his own, slightly less mythological time when he has Julius Caesar divinized to a star or comet by Jupiter's decree. Venus stands invisible in the Roman Senate:

And from her Caesar's body took his new expulsèd sprite,
The which she not permitting to resolve to aïr quite,
Did place it in the sky among the stars that glister bright,
And as she bare it, she did feel it gather heavenly might,
And for to waxen fiery. She no sooner let it fly,
But that a goodly shining star it up aloft did stye [mount]
And drew a great way after it bright beams like burning hair . . .

(*Metamorphosis*, XV. 948–56)[19]

So, in Shakespeare's *1 Henry VI*, Bedford tells the future Henry V 'A far more glorious star thy soul will make | Than Julius Caesar, or bright . . . '.[20] Or, turning to visual art, the Caesarean deification is found in Louis Laguerre's Chatsworth Hall mural of 1694. These instances belong to the

---

[18] Probably as part of the Callimachian vogue. Cf. Samuel Butler, *Hudibras*, II. iii. 844; Mildmay Fane, 'Sapiens Dominabitur', *ad fin.*: Fulbeck MS 'Poems 1655'; and Fontenelle, who gives Berenice a prominent part in *Dialogues of the Dead*, II. vi.

[19] Trans. Arthur Golding, from *Metam.* 15. 840–8: Ovid (1961: 313). Cf. Virgil, *Aen.* 8. 681; *Eclogues* 9. 47. For the relation of the Caesarian comet to the divinization of Augustus, see Syme (1960: 318).

[20] I. i. 56; cf. *Romeo and Juliet*, III. ii. 21, *Pericles*, V. iii. 79. Cf. the 1570 device of the printer Clément Baudin, showing a new star shooting to heaven from the altar of Clementia, with the *mot* MICAT INTER OMNES IULIUM SIDUS: see Butsch (1969, pl. 130).

register of political panegyric, like Donne's injunction to Princess Elizabeth in his 1613 epithalamium—'Be thou a new star, that to us portends | Ends of much wonder'— where the stellification is to be achieved by wearing a constellation of wedding jewels.[21] Merely charming as the latter example may seem, to reduce it altogether to social politics would underestimate both the persistence of ancient metaphysics and the strength of Renaissance beliefs in stellification.

Virgil added his authority in one of the most influential passages in ancient literature, *Georgics* I. 32, where he imagines that Augustus 'may add himself as a new star or constellation . . . where, between Virgo and the grasping Claws [of Scorpio], a space is opening'. In the Middle Ages, as we shall see in the next chapter, stellification generally followed this Virgilian plan of aggrandizing national champions with quasi-imperial claims. It was a destiny for the great, like Arthur. The exception of Chaucer proves this rule, for he is terrified to think he may have been seized upon for the stellification of celebrity.[22] Such ascensions sat awkwardly with Christian doctrine, and one may guess them to be vestiges, in part, of older star worship surviving as a popular under-cult. But prayer to animate stars had also the intellectual authority of figures like Jabir Ibn Hayyan. It lingered on as an esoteric tradition—as witness the *Picatrix*, available in Hebrew and Latin translations.[23]

In fact there was much vagueness about the nature of stars, which the medieval habit of allegorical thought did nothing to dispel. It encouraged extension of the biblical metaphors associating people with stars. Thus *The Golden Legend* slides easily between allegorical and physical senses of Revelation 8: 'the stars shall be said to fall, because they cast out rays of fire, or because there be many that seem clear as stars and then shall fall from the faith'.[24] Meanwhile, a less allegorical,

[21] Graham Parry (1981: 105).   [22] *The Hous of Fame*, 584–99.

[23] *DSB* vii. 42a. For a recent edition, see Pingree (1986). Pingree is also the author of several other not always dependable books and articles on medieval astrology, such as *The Thousands of Abu Màhar* (1968).

[24] Voragine (1900: i. 13; cf. ii. 124).

almost material conception of stellar afterlife could be arrived at through misunderstanding of stoic passages accepting mortality. In a celebrated dialogue Seneca offers Marcia the consolation that her dead husband and son 'are pervious to the matter of the stars, and, in turn, are mingled with it' (*pervii sunt intermixtique sideribus*)[25]—merely an expression, probably, of the widespread need to merge with the cosmos at death.

Several early Church Fathers held the stars to be animate; and Origen developed the idea that the resurrection body was a stellar 'principle' of the mortal body. Accepted by St Ambrose, this doctrine was misinterpreted by others as purely spiritual resurrection, and so at first rejected. But opposition to it failed in the longer run. The stars' animation became a medieval assumption, although one frequently challenged and gradually weakened, until at last it was assailable.[26]

The New Science

During the Renaissance, interest in stellification intensified greatly. For Pythagoreanism enjoyed an extraordinary revival among both intellectuals and people of fashion, and brought with it aspiration to the uncorrupted purity of the stars. Meanwhile, major developments in astronomy were dramatically changing the frontiers of mutable and immutable. It would be hard to exaggerate the emotional and speculative significance attaching to the great innovations—Copernicus' hypothesis that earth was a star (that is, a planet); Galileo's

[25] *Dialogi VI; Ad Marciam de Consolatione* 25. 3. The satiric deification in the *Apocolocyntosis* (Pumpkinification of Claudius) should not be taken to imply scepticism about stellification.

[26] On de-animation, see A. B. Scott (1991: 151–2, 166); Dales (1980); Blumenberg (1987). It was still incomplete in the late 17th century: the deist Charles Blount describes comets as 'dead bodies of the fixed stars, unburied': Blount (1695: 63). Similarly, the notion of stars feeding lingered on: e.g. *Divine Weeks*, I. iv. 101–6: Du Bartas (1979: i. 209); Milton, *Paradise Lost*, v. 469–98.

lunar mountains; and, above all, the *maculae*, or flaws, in the sun.[27] Sunspots seemed to prove the sun's corruptibility, an idea that badly upset the scientific establishment. To oppose it, Christopher Scheiner was prepared to posit dark stars interposing between sun and observer.[28]

We tend to think of Copernicus' and Galileo's discoveries as 'advances' leading to the world-picture of modern science. But for their contemporaries the new science had very different implications. Moon-mountains, for example, could be exaggerated into a habitable, quasi-terrestrial landscape, and taken to substantiate ancient fancies about a lunar origin of nobility. This notion is to be met with in a Winchester textbook of the sixteenth century;[29] to say nothing of Shakespeare's Hotspur, admittedly no intellectual, who thinks 'To pluck bright honour from the pale-faced moon'.[30] Alternatively, the lunar landscape might corroborate the view that the dead inhabit the moon,[31] a Plutarchian doctrine which was to interest Cromwell's brother-in-law Bishop Wilkins, unofficial head of the Royal Society.

The interruptions telescopy revealed in stellar surfaces were so many loopholes in the boundary walls of mortality—openings to the immortal world above. Formerly the moon's orbit had been the unqualified divider between mortality and immortality, mutability and immutability: 'All, all is mine beneath moon's silver sphere,' claims Drummond's Death.[32] Now, this was relativized. One should not say the frame of the

---

[27] Tufte (1990: 18). On Harriott's anticipation of Galileo, see North (1989: 109–44).   [28] Scheiner (1613).

[29] *Hieroglyphica* (1556) XL. xxiii, 'Nobilitas': Valeriano (1613: 560–1). In 1641 John Evelyn was 'confirmed in my opinion of the moon's being of such a substance as this earthly globe; perceiving all the subjacent country (at so small an horizontal distance) to repercuss such a light as I could hardly look against, save where the river and other large waters appeared of a more dark and even surface, exceedingly resembling the spots in the moon according to that of Hevelius, and as they appear in our late telescopes': Evelyn (1955: i. 43–4 and ii. 64).

[30] *1 Henry IV*, I. iii. 202. Cf. the *pseudodoxion* that pelicans migrate from the moon; see Mundy (1907–36: v. 157).   [31] Cumont (1922: 93).

[32] Fowler (1991: 259).

medieval world-picture was broken. But there was certainly blurring of its mutable and immutable registers. The afterlife had somehow become more tangible. Translunary things were almost accessible. 'If the heavens then be penetrable . . . and no lets', remarks Robert Burton, 'it were not amiss in this aerial progress to make wings and fly up.'[33] This is not so very far from the mood of Spenser's Dame Mutabilitie when she climbs to the circle of the moon to challenge Cynthia where she 'raignes in everlasting glory' (VII. vi. 8), and to claim sovereignty over all the planetary gods.

Even to those less overreaching than Dame Mutabilitie, the new astronomy suggested exciting possibilities for the afterlife. Pico's *De Hominis Dignitate* had challenged mankind to ascend beyond the stars in a spiritual sense—to aspire, in effect, to sanctification.[34] A century later, the challenge was taken up more literally. With the seventeenth-century reversion to the Greek and early Latin Fathers, Origen's stellar afterlife had its own vigorous *Nachleben*. Even Kepler thought that 'the elliptical trajectory of the planets was a "declining" form of circular perfection'—an odd perpetuation of Origen's sinful stars.[35] How far conceptions of stellar ascesis had changed from Pico's time may be gauged by Galileo's black joke of 1613: he hoped that his recently deceased opponent, who had refused to look through a telescope while on earth, would pay attention to the new celestial objects while on his way to heaven.[36]

Cosmic enlargement excited in some a romantic enthusiasm for 'brave [splendid] translunary things';[37] the sense of man's infinitude prompted affirmations like Sir Philip Sidney's, of the poet's subjective power to range 'within the zodiac of his own wit'. ('Zodiac' became a vogue word, as

---

[33] *Anatomy of Melancholy*, II. ii. 3. i: Burton (1989– : ii. 48).

[34] Pico is unlikely to have had astrological notions in mind here: he was the author of *Disputationes adversus Astrologiam Divinatricem*: Mirandola (1973).

[35] Maiorino (1990: 128). Blount (1695: 63) similarly thinks that the sun's spots show 'him' to be sick.   [36] Drake (1957: 73): cit. Tufte (1990: 20).

[37] Drayton on Marlowe, 'Epistle to Reynolds', line 106 (1931–41: iii. 228).

book-titles of the period testify.[38]) In others, enlargement took the shape of ambition for empire.[39] Universally, however, the new science entailed rethinking the limits of the cosmos.[40] The medieval *sphaera stellata*, the crystal orb of 'fixed' stars, had become problematic. 'Tycho hath feigned', writes Burton, 'I know not how many subdivisions of epicycles in epicycles, etc. to calculate and express the moon's motion; but when all is done, as a supposition, and no otherwise; not (as he holds) hard, impenetrable, subtile, transparent, . . . but still [always] quiet, liquid, open, etc.'[41] Telescopic observation, it might be held, had eliminated the bounding sphere by revealing stars too distant to be visible before. Or, as Kepler and others correctly argued, the newly revealed stars might be small rather than distant.[42]

Aspiration, or wishfulness, discerned amid these uncertainties many new reasons for hope. The idea began to be entertained that ordinary people, not just emperors, might partake of stellar substance and find niches among the stars. One need not see this as a recrudescence of paganism. It may suggest Stoicism and neo-Pythagoreanism. But by then Pythagorean ideas had long been accommodated both to astronomical thought and to Christian doctrine.[43] This is especially

[38] e.g. Marcello Palingenio, *Zodiacus Vitae* (1574); Caspar von Barth, *Zodiacus Vitae* (1623); Philippus van der Beken, *Zodiacus Religiosus* (1669); Nicolas de Blégny, *Zodiacus Medico-Gallicus* (1680–5); Bartholomaeus Christelius, *Zodiacus Laetofatalis* (1690); and many others. Wenceslas Hollar provided etchings for *The Christian's Zodiac* (London, 1643, 1647), an English translation of Hieremias Drexelius' *Zodiacus Christianus* (1618), a work that has little substantively to do with astronomy (Drexelius 1978). During the 17th century, numbers of titles introducing the word 'zodiac' and its derivatives probably reached three figures.

[39] W. Kerrigan and G. Braden, (1989, ch. 7, esp. pp. 124–5).

[40] As Koyré (1958) explains in convincing detail.

[41] *Anatomy of Melancholy*, II. ii. 3. i: Burton (1989– : ii. 48).

[42] Burton (1989– : ii. 77; cf. 94).

[43] The importance of Pythagorean ideas from the early Renaissance to the end of the 17th century is hard to exaggerate. See Heninger (1968, 1974: 58, 67, and *passim*), reviewed unfavourably by Hardison (1977); *The Cambridge History of Renaissance Philosophy* (1988), index, s.v. *Pythagoreanism* and *Neopythagoreanism*, esp. 204; Burkert (1973); Drake (1970); Palisca (1956); Philip (1966). Thomas Stanley devoted many pages of his *History of Philosophy* to what he supposed were

true of Calvinism; but in Catholic tradition, too, the meritorious elect might become angels in the afterlife.[44] The stars had long been guided by 'Intelligences', or angelic spirits; now these spiritual Intelligences, demoted by Reformed theology and multiplied by telescopic observation, offered *loci* for personal immortality.

Hopes of stellification are expressed with striking frequency. They underlie, for example, George Herbert's familiar but misunderstood verse 'The stars have us to bed'.[45] And Lord Herbert, in 'To His Mistress for Her True Picture', adds stars to the conventional robe of death.[46] When Sarbiewski's solitary contemplates the stars he weeps for joy and

> through his tears
> Looks on the fire-enamelled spheres,
> Where with his Saviour he would be
> Lifted above mortality.

('The Praise of a Religious Life by Mathias Casimirus', lines 25–8)[47]

And an anonymous elegist consoles Mr Persall for the loss of his little daughter at Amsterdam in 1658 with the reflection that her 'pure spirit' is now in 'its proper sphere'; the parents should not mourn their 'pretty messenger of love', their 'new intelligence above'.[48]

Surely the greatest poetic stellification of the century is Jonson's Cary–Morison ode, in which the reciprocity and mutual sacrifice of friendship finds a profound analogy in the alternate setting and rising of the twin 'asterism' Gemini, mythologized as Castor and Pollux. Details of the imagery beautifully enact the stellification: at the poem's

Pythagoras' ideas. Pythagoreanism was not always pursued at an esoteric level: instructional Pythagorean games were played in Italian academies, such as Innocenzio Ringhieri's 'Giuoco dei numeri' and Benedetto Varchi's 'Il Giuoco di Pitagora'; see Watson (1993: 63, 103, 204–5).

[44] e.g. Voragine (1900: v. 195). For Calvin's comparison of risen souls to angels, see Kremen (1972: 72).   [45] 'Man', line 31: Herbert (1941: 91).

[46] See Farmer (1984: 41).   [47] Vaughan (1957: 90).

[48] 'On the Death of Mr Persall's Little Daughter in the Beginning of the Spring, at Amsterdam': Blunden and Mellor (1963).

numerological centre the 'lily of a day' becomes the 'flower of light'—a contemporary cognomen of Cygnus, which itself rises as Gemini sets.[49] The status of an entire constellation is similarly expected for Lord Hastings; the controversial vicar Samuel Bold (1649–1737) reviews Hastings' merits as doctor, virgin, and martyr, then delivers a valediction that hovers between glory, fame, and the constellations Corona Borealis and Australis:

> Hie then, immortal soul, to thine own sphere,
> Where these three crowns attend thee; and shine there
> A glorious constellation, far above
> The frowns of fortune, or the pangs of love.
>
> ('A Funeral Elegy . . . ', *ad fin.*)[50]

And when Katherine Philips dies, J.C. promises that 'Her sacred dust, calcined by time, shall be | The richest filings of high poesy', until 'Her all dispersed, at last shall meet in one, | And shine a glorious constellation.'[51] Davenant's Lover, more humbly—or perhaps more mindful of Kepler's argument about faint stars—expects his dying mistress only to 'add light to some small star . . . every mistress, when she dies, | Is changed at least into a star'; although his Philosopher, agnostic as Jeremy Taylor, cautions 'ask not bodies doomed to die | To what abode they go'.[52] Henry Vaughan, the poet of light, has several stellifications, most notably 'They are all gone into the world of light', with its adaptation of the contemporary myth of inextinguishable lamps in tombs:

[49] R. H. Allen (1963: 194); on Spenser's use of the association, see Fowler (1975: 68). Cf. Euripides, *Orestes* 1683–5 and 1635–7 ('Helen lives . . . and now, between Castor and Pollux she sits enthroned . . . a star of deliverance for sailors'). Helen shared a cult with the Dioscuri.

[50] B[rome] (1649: 34). Cf. Samuel Woodforde's verses before Walton's 'Life of Herbert': 'Let his great name from Earth by raised on high, | And in the starry volume of the sky | A lasting record find: | Be with his mighty psaltery joined; | Which, taken long since up into the air, | And called the Harp, makes a bright constellation there': I. Walton (1973: 254).

[51] Thorn-Drury (1921: 28). Probably J.C. is John Crouch.

[52] Davenant (1972: 175).

> If a star were confined into a Tomb
> Her captive flames must needs burn there;
> But when the hand that locked her up, gives room,
> She'll shine through all the sphere.

('Ascension—Hymn', lines 29–32)[53]

In the Restoration, still, 'The blessed Saints that watched this turning Scene | Did from their Stars with joyful wonder lean';[54] but more often, now, stellification dwindles to perfunctory commonplaces and vapid apotheoses.

It was in fact a convention of elegy to describe the subject 'in terms of heavenly bodies'.[55] An idea so common naturally invited witty variation: John Evelyn sees Cowley, like Ovid's Medea, 'mount and with his head | Strike the bright sphere';[56] Crashaw exalts the dead St Theresa as 'the moon of maiden stars';[57] and Marvell puns on shooting stars—many Fairfaxes and Veres 'fell in war, | Yet more to heaven shooting are'.[58] In the visual arts similar conventions obtained, starry crowns similarly abounded. The celestial globe common on seventeenth-century title-pages and in Dutch still lifes (usually interpreted in *vanitas* terms as indicating the universality of transience) perhaps as often refers specifically to stellification.[59]

The question naturally now arises (although it would not

---

[53] Vaughan (1957: 484), probably taking a suggestion from Jacob Cats's proverb-emblem VERITÀ NON PUO STAR SEPOLTA (Truth cannot stay buried): see Praz (1964: 227–8), illus. in Rogers (1987: 185). Cf. Vaughan (1957: 59), weakening stellification to similitude: 'as some Star | Hurled in Diurnal motions from far, | And seen to droop at night, is vainly said | To fall, and find an Occidental bed, | Though in that other world what we Judge West | Proves Elevation, and a new, fresh East'. On the tomb lamp myth, see Piggott (1976: 88).

[54] Dryden, *Astraea Redux*, lines 153–4 (1958: i. 20).

[55] Murphy (1972: 78). The convention persisted, in attenuated form, into the 18th century: e.g. 'Is H[unter] dead, and nothing in the sky | As it does justice to the glorious dead?' (John Lumby, 1728: Bodl. MS Eng. poet. e. 42, fol. 36).

[56] Ovid, *Metam.* 8. 61.

[57] 'A Hymn to the Name and Honour of the Admirable Saint Teresa . . . ', line 123.   [58] 'Upon Appleton House', st. lxii; cf. st. lxxxvi.

[59] e.g. Ember (1989, no. 21, Jan van der Heyden, and no. 30, K. Lux). See Morgan (1983).

have arisen in the Renaissance) whether some of the passages quoted above are not merely metaphorical. Clearly there is a difference between, on the one hand, fully developed affirmations of metaphysic belief, and, on the other, brief applications of stellar metaphors for literary purposes. And it may be supposed that in general a clear distinction can be made between the two: between 'mere metaphors' and passages implying religious beliefs—or, at least, from which definite metaphysics are to be extracted. But I have come to think that this is a misconception, based on inappropriate notions of seventeenth-century thought and language. For one thing, all metaphors, then as now, contain metaphysical assumptions, usually unexamined.[60] For another, it is easy to mistake brief mentions of stars as having a purely rhetorical function, when they would have been taken up differently by readers sharing earlier domains of assumption. There is, of course, a range of seriousness, and of conscious engagement with metaphysics. Few would doubt that in the quoted passages Sarbiewski and Vaughan, and the poet of the Persall elegy, express actual beliefs. At another extreme, the Cowley, like the Crashaw, and perhaps the Bold and Woodforde, may all seem metaphorical passages—until, that is, one recalls other passages of Cowley, with their highly developed imagery of alchemic ascesis. When Crashaw, exhorting the Countess of Denbigh to overcome her religious doubts, calls on 'Almighty love [to] end this long war, | And of a meteor make a star',[61] this is indeed forceful rhetoric. But its full persuasiveness is missed unless one recalls that Crashaw associates the stars with risen souls—as in 'The Weeper' xii:

> When some new bright guest
> Takes up among the stars a room,
> And heaven will make a feast.   (st. xii)[62]

Herbert and especially Jonson have their eye on the poetic possibilities of stellification; yet there is no reason to suppose they were any less serious about its literal possibility as a

[60] See Lakoff and Johnson (1980).   [61] Crashaw (1927: 237).
[62] Crashaw (1927: 310).

religious hope. In short, it is often impossible to know how to make this unreal distinction, so that it may sometimes be best to remain agnostic. Probably fewer than we suppose of Renaissance stellifications were merely metaphorical (whatever that means).

Places in the Sun

There was surprisingly little scepticism about what one might expect many to have regarded as false surmise. Expressions of stellar aspiration were accepted as a matter of course in the seventeenth century. In the sceptical century before, however, they had sometimes attracted ideological derision. We have noticed Foxe's reference to papal 'stellification'—although he might not have been so scornful if stellification of the elect had been in question. Another doughty Reformer, William Harrison, author of 'The Description of Britain' prefaced to Holinshed's *Chronicle*, attacked the whole notion as pagan and (what to him was far worse) smacking of papist hagiolatry. Reducing it euhemeristically, he explains that stellified heroes and planetary gods were translated mentally to the stars by the society honouring them.[63] With revealing inconsistency, though, he adds an argument from overcrowding that treats the 'translation in heaven' as real: 'every of those that were called gods, could not obtain that benefit, for then should there not have been stars enow [enough] in heaven'.[64] This repeats a gibe of the early Christian Bishop Eusebius of Alexandria, who asked 'were there only two stars in the time

[63] Drayton may have Harrison in mind when he writes that the stars were named 'By those wise ancients, not to stellify | The first world's heroes only, but imply | To reach their courses' ('The Man in the Moon', lines 465–7: Drayton 1931–41: ii. 586).

[64] 'The Description of Britain': Harrison (1807: 38); see G. J. R. Parry (1987). Scepticism in the later 17th century may be exemplified by poor Arthur Brett's 'Stellification, Fancy Is', *Threnodia* (1660: 19). On earlier star worship in Britain, see Thomas (1988: 203); on vagueness in ideas of the afterlife, Thomas (1988: 194); on the limited number of noble places available, Plumb (1969: 35 n.).

of Adam and Eve? . . . and eight after the Flood when Noah and seven other persons alone were saved in the Ark?'[65] Celestial places were as limited as the number of the stars. Was not the total of the fixed stars itself fixed? It was set down in Ptolemy's star catalogue as 1,022. And in Aristotle's view the number of Intelligences (as distinct from 'gods') was limited more stringently still to eight, the count of the spheres they guided.[66] If places were so few, what hope did stellification offer?

Here the new science fortunately intervened. The astronomer Tycho Brahe, returning home one November evening, noticed a bright star shining in a part of the sky where none should have been. Ever the cautious observer, he compared notes with his servants and with some passing country folk. Then he made notes on the 1572 nova.[67] This observation is sometimes said to have overthrown Ptolemaic astronomy and its associated world-picture. Looked at in the long term this may almost be true—and in the short term, so far as astronomers were concerned. To these, the nova called much in doubt. But to many others the nova had no such significance. It might, indeed, arouse fears of an astrological nature, or even seem an omen of apocalypse.[68] But it was just as likely to seem an auspicious miracle confirming the providential view of history. Immediately the nova became a subject for religious poetry,[69] and in 1638 the Protestant emblemist Quarles was still celebrating it. In one of his epigrams, the nova

[65] Cumont (1922: 92); cf. Rathborne (1937: 142), and the popular anonymous *Pantagruel's Prognostication* (1947: 21–2).
[66] *Metaphysica* 12. 8, a familiar passage in the Renaissance: e.g. Pomponazzi (1948: 367).
[67] Quarles (1960: 42); Kuhn (1985: 206–9); Nicolson (1985: 116–19). On Brahe, see Thoren (1990); Dreyer (1953).   [68] Nicolson (1985: 120).
[69] e.g. Richard Wills, *Poematum Liber*, XXII, 'De Stella quae Anno 1572 in Extremo Caepta est Videri Iuxta Cassiopaeam': Wills (1573: 16). Comparing the nova to the star of Bethlehem, Wills calms astrological fears—it is not ominous universally, since being in a northern sign it cannot affect the Ethiopians.

resembles that earlier new star, the star of Bethlehem. In another, it is that, and also a miracle to move belief:

> Let them not boast that they first saw this star,
> A brawny brainless clown might go as far,
> The star in Cassiopea as I find
> Ticho confess, was showed him by a hind.
> Wise though they were, they'd gone they knew not whether,
> Had this star then been sent to lead them thither.
> So that the star which did before them go
> Both showed them light, and showed their blindness too.
> But why a star? When God doth mean to woo us,
> He useth means that are familiar to us.
>
> ('Of the Wise Men', lines 1–10)[70]

The nova showed, moreover, that if stellification called for additional stars this need not be a difficulty. Together with the new astronomy's previously invisible faint stars it offered a solution to the problem of accommodating the resurrected. It was a discovery revealing the way to a stellar afterlife.

The notion of people dying into stars may seem bizarrely naïve. But allowance needs to be made for the naturalizing, externalizing thrust of both Renaissance and Reformation. When contemplative spirituality was largely abandoned, a few Neoplatonists like Pico continued to write of ascesis in quasi-mystical terms. But, for the most part, intellectual Christians seem to have looked for a more tangible ladder of ascent. Some found it in alchemy, others in contemplation of natural forms (symbols, now, of divinity), others again in emotional struggles for salvation—in the wrestling of Eros with Anteros. In such circumstances a hope understandably grew of realizing the spiritual body of Pauline theology by ascent to the incorruptible (or less corrupted) stars. Might not the flame of zeal merge in some sense, literal or spiritual, with

---

[70] Quarles (1960: 6–7); on the poem's date see p. x. Kepler interpreted the star of Bethlehem as 'an initial conjunction in the fiery trigon, comparable with the one in 1603', and also compared the nova of 1604: *De Vero Anno* (1614): cit. *DSB* vii. 298.

stellar fire? Quarles likens the flames of Pentecost to stars 'with which th' Apostles were all stellified'. He assigns astronomical locality: they were 'turned to the twelve Signs, through which the sun | Of righteousness should as his zodiac run'.[71]

Purer Fire

The precise means of stellification, however, remained obstinately elusive. Some appear to have tried regimens of purification. Sir John Harington (to whom we owe not only the invention of the water-closet but many keen observations of court mores) scorns luxurious livers who hope nevertheless for stellification. Ancient Pythagorean astronomers dieted to improve their sight, and 'called this sparing diet, stellifying':[72]

> thinkest thou, professèd Epicure,
> That never couldest virtuous pains endure,
> That eatst fat ven'son, boozest claret wine . . .
> That thou art worthy to be stellified?

('Of One that Seeks to Be Stellified Being No Pythagorean', lines 11–16)

Perhaps Milton thinks Thomas Randolph similarly self-deceiving when he echoes Randolph's 'We whose souls are made of purer fire' in Comus' opening song: 'We that are of purer fire | Imitate the starry choir.' There is no irony, though, in T.B.'s assurance in 1636 that John Dyke's soul

> rapt with desire,
> Disdains dull Earth, and aims at glories higher:
> And by a bright Angelic fire enflamed,
> Mounts towards heaven, as oft as hears it named.

('To the Truly Worthy. . . Mrs Judith Dyke', lines 19–22)[73]

---

[71] Quarles (1960: 21). Cf. Cowley's elegy comparing William Hervey to 'the stars, to which he now is gone, | That shine with beams like flame, | Yet burn not with the same': Cowley (1905: 35).

[72] *Epigrams*, i. 68, 'Of One That Seeks to Be Stellified Being No Pythagorean': Harington (1930: 174, no. 69).   [73] Beedome (1928: 33).

By an opposite error to Comus', some of austerer bent simplified stellification to discipline. They tried to put off the flesh—to put off, even, the lower soul. It may surprise the reader to find something of this in John Donne, the supposed celebrator of passion. Nevertheless, it is Donne's 'dull sublunary lovers . . . Whose soul is sense'; his ideal lover is refined into the semblance of an angel, or spiritual Intelligence in its sphere.[74] William Habington, similarly, reminds Castara about Calisto's and Leda's stellifications, and invites her to find with him 'a pure and glorious sphere':

> If each of these loose beauties are
> Transformed to a more beauteous star
> By the adult'rous lust of Jove,
> Why should not we, by purer love?
>
> ('To Castara', lines 23–6)[75]

He wishes to 'fix like stars for ever there'.

Others pursued stellification through some sort of Paracelsian or alchemic purification. In the elegy for Persall's daughter quoted earlier, it was 'heaven's almighty chemic [alchemist]' who had 'Drawn this pure spirit to its proper sphere'. And in Cowley's 'The Ecstasy' Elijah, 'that second man', ascends beyond the planets in a wondrous coach symbolic of the alchemist's art:

> 'Twas gaudy all, and rich in every part,
> Of essences of gems, and spirit of gold
>   Was its substantial mould;
>   Drawn forth by chemic angels' art
> Here with moonbeams 'twas silvered bright,
> There double-gilt with the sun's light
>   And mystique shapes cut round in it,
> Figures that did transcend a vulgar angel's wit. (st. viii)[76]

---

[74] 'Valediction Forbidding Mourning', 13 ff.; cf. 'Air and Angels'. For the stellified as Intelligences, cf. Pomponazzi (1948: 367); Cowley, *Davideidos*, i. 67.

[75] Habington (1938: 63).

[76] Cowley (1905: 205). Cf. the anonymous 'Upon the New Invention of Flying with Chymical Magic': Anon. (1659: 79); also Basilius Valentinus (1962).

(Who but Cowley would imagine superiority over angelic wit?) Such vehicular ascents may be related to Ovid's stellification of Hercules in a chariot—*quadriiugo curru radiantibus intulit astris*—allegorized by Christianizing neo-Stoics like Charles de Langhe as a model for the garden-philosopher's ascent above the body's limitations in the chariot of wisdom (*Sapientiae quadrigis*).[77] In the seventeenth century the ascent became more scientific, the vehicle being now specifically alchemic, like that in the *Triumph-Wagen Antimonii* . . . (1604) of Basilius Valentinus, the Benedictine Friar.[78]

It is possible that many seventeenth-century mentions of stellification are influenced by alchemic ideas. With the large, and largely distinct, system of alchemy, however, we cannot be concerned here. Nevertheless, it needs to be kept in mind throughout our more astronomical enquiry that where stellification was meant metaphorically, the metaphor is quite likely to have had an alchemical (psychodynamic) dimension.

Planetary Afterlives

For those who found mortification daunting and the psychodynamics of alchemic ascesis impalpable, there was a more material alternative. Stellification could be imagined in terms of space travel. Here again the new astronomy played an exciting part. Neo-Pythagoreans had for a century speculated that the planets might be accessible worlds; now speculation was given observational substance by the astronomers. Perhaps the most influential were John Wilkins and Christiaan Huygens.[79] But writers of every calibre were ready to imagine planets as worlds. It seems best to give a range of examples. William Hammond (fl. 1655–85):

---

[77] *Metam.* 9. 262–72; Morford (1987: 163 and n. 82).
[78] Basilius Valentinus (1660).
[79] Wilkins (1638 etc.); Huygens (1698 etc.). See Stanley (1660: i. 101); Bachrach (1962); Guthke (1991).

You modern wits, who call this world a star,
Who say the other planets, too, worlds are,
And that the spots that in the midst are found
Are to the people there islands and ground;
And that the water which surrounds the Earth
Reflects to each, and gives their shining birth . . .

('The Tears', lines 1–6)[80]

Margaret Cavendish, who knew a good deal of science, wonders 'who doth know, but stars we see by night | Are suns which to some other worlds give light?'[81] Thomas Heyrick (1649–94), curate of Market Harborough and amateur scientist, unnecessarily reminds the sun:

Thou dost i' th' moon and planets shine;
And, if astronomy say true,
Our Earth to them doth seem a planet too.

('On a Sunbeam', lines 6–8)[82]

The strong Copernican Robert Wittie (1613?–84) aims in his *Ouranoskopia* (1681) to show 'the probability of more inhabited worlds' and 'to prove the sun to be the seat of the blessed, with several other useful notions'. Some divines had put the afterlife 'above the starry heaven', but 'that is an immeasurable space, and methink not so suitable for finite beings'. Others favoured the planets, but since these are 'perhaps of the same nature . . . as this Earth, they seem not . . . so fit for glorified beings'. In opting for a solar location, it counts with Wittie that the sun is 'centre of the heavens'. Bishop Wilkins is noticeably more agnostic, although he allows that the Plutarchian heaven in the moon is 'some such place as we suppose paradise to be'.[83]

Undoubtedly the most popular exposition of planetary astronomy was *Entretiens sur la pluralité des mondes* (1686) by Bernard le Bovier de Fontenelle (1657–1757). An immediate

---

[80] Saintsbury (1905: ii. 517).   [81] 'Of Stars', lines 7–8: Fowler (1991: 631).
[82] Fowler (1991: 761–2).
[83] Wilkins (1972: 199). Cf. W. Smith (1688)—William Smith (b. 1615 or 1616), a prebendary of Norwich.

best-seller, this middlebrow Copernican and Cartesian popularization rapidly disseminated mechanistic ideas of astronomy throughout Europe.[84] Fontenelle held the planets to be
habitable, influenced in this by Wilkins's *Discovery of a New
World* (1638), which had been translated into French in 1655.[85]
Fontenelle was no astronomer, and his engaging dialogue
cannot claim to be profound. But it was opportune in sketch-
ing ideas of stellar habitation plausibly enough to make them
imaginable in physical detail. He succeeded in turning the
popular conception of stellification into distinctly material
avenues. Fontenelle and Wittie are within measurable distance, in fact, of Arthur Clarke and Stanley Kubrick's *2001*,
if the latter may be taken to illustrate a conception of stellar
afterlife imaginable in our own century.

Terrestrial Afterlife

We may seem to have come down to very externalized,
unspiritual conceptions of the afterlife. But ideas still more
mundane were current. William Harrison's account of early
British religion, mentioned earlier, distinguishes three separate destinations after death. Princes and heroes might hope
for a 'place in heaven, among the shining stars'; but there
were not enough stars for all, so that 'another place was in
time imagined' where the Semones, or minor deities,
reigned.[86] And there was also 'a third place, that is to say

---

[84] Soon there were many editions, and translations into English by H. A.
Hargreaves (1688 etc.), Aphra Behn (1688 etc.), John Glanvill (1688 etc.),
William Gardiner (1715 etc.). About twenty-six British editions appeared in
the 18th century. See Fontenelle (1955, 1990).

[85] Wilkins's *Discovery* (1638) was itself perhaps prompted by Francis Godwin's
Man in the Moon (1638); both envisaged space flight. Cf. also Pierre Borel, *Discours
nouveau prouvant la pluralité des mondes* (1657); Cyrano de Bergerac, *L'Autre Monde:
L'Histoire comique des états et empires de la lune* (1657) and *L'Histoire comique des états et
empires du soleil* (1662); Hans Jakob Christoffel von Grimmelshausen, *Simplicissimus*
(1659). See Fontenelle (1955, 1990); *DSB*.

[86] 'The Description of Britain'; Harrison (1807: 38); on the Semones, see
Fulgentius (1971: 164).

an Earth, where those gods dwelt which were noble men, officers, good governors and lawgivers to the people, and yet not thought worthy to be of the second or first company'. That, sneers the egalitarian Harrison, 'was a jolly division'. The third vision, of immortality on earth (or 'an earth'), faded like the others after the conversion of Britain. But it had a dramatic revival in seventeenth-century millenarianism. The apocalyptic prophecy that Christ would return to rule on earth for a thousand years was not a new one. It seemed to have the authority, indeed, of biblical texts. But chiliasm had drenched so many centuries in blood that mainstream Reformers and Romanists avoided it carefully; interpreting 'a thousand years' as 'a long time', 'indefinitely', 'time without end', or even 'eternity'.[87] Others were less circumspect, however, so that a new recrudescence of millenarianism ensued.

As for Milton, the *De Doctrina* is anything but circumspect: it sounds the trumpet of an uncompromisingly literal millenarian apocalypse.[88] Yet in *Paradise Lost*, C. A. Patrides argues, Milton draws back from millenarianism.[89] How resolve this contradiction? Patrides is right, so far as positive commitment goes. But a contrary suggestion may be detected in Raphael's visionary prognostication of how obedient mankind's spiritualized (stellified?) bodies, 'improved by tract of time', may 'winged ascend', or 'at choice | Here or in heavenly paradises dwell'.[90] All this is to happen in a paradise never lost—in a hypothetical unfallen time-line—not in our own historical world. Nevertheless, it reveals much about Milton's vision of immortality: particularly the simultaneous materialism and spirituality, ranging 'at choice' between heaven and earth.

[87] Patrides (1966: 278–9).
[88] I. xxxiii: Yale Prose Milton, vi. 624–5. Cf. Patrides and Wittreich (1984: 226–7; Patrides (1966: 278–9).   [89] Patrides (1966: 227–31).
[90] *Paradise Lost*, v. 496–500; cf. *Il Penseroso*, 88–9, where Milton thinks to 'unsphere | The spirit of Plato'. Henry More, the Cambridge Platonist, argues that departed spirits enjoy the pleasures of landscape and terrestrial entertainments such as the theatre: More (1987: 213–14).

Milton's views contrast strikingly with Harrison's. The élitist Milton hopes that in the day of judgement 'those who [have] been earnest for the common good of religion and their country' will win decent places in the hierarchy, becoming angels or like angels: that, when Christ's 'mild monarchy through heaven and Earth' is established, they will

receive, above the inferior orders of the blessed, the regal addition of Principalities, Legions, and Thrones into their glorious titles, and in supereminence of beatific vision progressing the dateless and irrevoluble circle of eternity shall clasp inseparable hands with joy, and bliss in over measure for ever.[91]

Milton's terrestrial paradise is in keeping with his mortalism. For, like many of his time, he subscribed to the heresy that at death the soul shares the body's extinction, until both are resurrected together.[92] Quasi-millenarian as it is, his earthly paradise need not be thought eccentric. It was a widespread ideal in the seventeenth century, when science, mysticism, millenarianism, and reformist politics often combined in a strange, potentially explosive amalgam.[93] It continued to be a potent ideal, moreover, in nineteenth-century realizations such as utopian socialism and theology like James Walker's in *The Blessed Dead in Paradise* (1895).

The Nachleben *of Stellar Afterlife*

The later Milton interpreted paradise more inwardly— already Michael promises 'a paradise within thee, happier

[91] *Of Reformation*: Yale Prose Milton, i. 616. For the Renaissance metaphor of angelic *putti* and *puerili*, symbolizing the spirituality of regeneration, see Barolsky (1990: 119). Among 17th-century examples, cf. Thomas Carew, 'Maria Wentworth . . .', line 6 ('hatched a cherubin'): Carew (1957: 56).
[92] On mortalism, see Burns (1972); M. Y. Hughes (1965: 21 ff); and (on Sir Thomas Browne's attraction to it) W. Kerrigan and G. Braden (1989: 131 and 243 n. 16). Pomponazzi's 'On the Immortality of the Soul' was influential; see Pomponazzi (1948: 376).
[93] On Renaissance fascination with the whereabouts of the earthly paradise, see Prest (1981); Huet (1701).

far' (XII. 587). Comparably internalized is Cowley's alchemic stellification, with its metaphorical, scarcely mechanistic 'vehicle' of ascent. The alterity of such conceptions should not be exaggerated. In the course of mankind's long humanizing of nature, Renaissance people relate to the firmament much as the Romantic generation relates to landscape. Sometimes these two phases overlap, indeed, as in Wordsworth's 'Intimations of Immortality from Recollections of Early Childhood'. Identification with 'life's star' does not end abruptly; it gradually loses metaphysical validity. When stellification is alluded to in the nineteenth century, no more than sentiment, or sentimentality, seems to be implied. An instance of the first might be the famous *Lieder* by Heine, 'Es fällt ein Stern'; of the second, the speculations of Dickens's ridiculous Miggs, who 'wondered what star was destined for her habitation when she had run her little course below; perhaps speculated which of those glimmering spheres might be the natal orb of Mr Tappertit'.[94] Van Gogh probably means something comparably vague when he says 'Just as we take the train to get to Tarascon and Rouen, we take death to reach a star.'[95] In our own century, stellification may take the shape of science-fiction space travel, or out-of-the-body experiences such as Jung's stellar walkabout.[96] Only occasionally, as when Doris Lessing's Al·ith thinks 'stars are what we are made of ',[97] is something more like Pythagoreanism suggested.

The remarkable continuance of ideas of stellification can be viewed variously—as a pagan survival, for example, or as accommodation of certain biblical texts to successive stages of astronomy. Only by ignoring the evidence, however, could it be seen as an incomplete conquest of superstition by science. Almost the reverse is true. Belief in stellification raised problems which scientific discoveries time and again

[94] Heine (1827: Lyrisches Intermezzo lix; cf. xxii.3). Dickens (1986: 119).
[95] Cit. Westrich (1992: 24). [96] Jung (1963: 270).
[97] Lessing (1981: 240).

resolved, or seemed to resolve. As we have seen, it is not to be supposed that statements about stellification were 'merely' metaphorical—implying only that the elect were 'like stars'. That would beg the question how metaphorical and literal differed in seventeenth-century 'reality', besides ignoring the involvement of science itself with ideas of stellification. The ideal of the good life, as Milton imagines it in *Il Penseroso* and Pope in *Windsor-Forest*, is that of the Christian philosopher: a scientist (botanist, chemist, astronomer) who studies nature in the knowledge that the stars are somehow his destination. He

> looks on heav'n with more than mortal eyes,
> Bids his free soul expatiate in the skies,
> Amid her kindred stars familiar roam,
> Survey the region, and confess her home!
>
> (*Windsor-Forest*, lines 253–6)[98]

This idealizing mode of thought should not itself be idealized, however. Stellification was not always without political implications. We shall next explore its links with social structures and the pursuit of fame.

[98] The whole passage, lines 237–56, is relevant; see Røstvig (1971: ii. 58–9).

3

Trumpets and Asterisms

I've paid thee what I promised. That's not all:
Besides, I give thee here a verse that shall
(When hence thy circum-mortal-part is gone)
Arch-like, hold up thy name's inscription.
Brave men can't die, whose candid actions are
Writ in the poet's endless calendar;
Whose velum and whose volume is the sky,
And the pure stars the praising poetry.
Farewell

(Robert Herrick, 'To His Peculiar Friend
Master Thomas Shapcott, Lawyer')

When I was a child, school exercises used sometimes to be handed back with gold stars affixed, like Michelin Guide seals of approval; and 'star treatment' is still accorded to pop 'stars'. The term goes back before film and circus stars to the theatrical world of 1779, when (according to John Heneage Jesse) Garrick dimmed all the little stars. Earlier still, George Chapman called Mary Wroth 'the happy star discovered in our Sidneyan asterism' or constellation.[1] When 'stellify' meant 'praise', 'stars' were 'cynosures'.

In the information age, fame can seem less metaphysical and more self-fulfilling. When the noise is the message, the burden of Fame's trumpet may be no more than 'these are famous because I blow their trumpet'. (If, indeed, they do not blow it themselves.[2]) Alternatively, the famous may be those

---

[1] *The* Iliads *of Homer* (1611), Sig. Gg 4^v.

[2] On which practice, see Shakespeare, *Much Ado*, v. ii. 73, from Cicero, *De Oratore* 2. 20. 86 ('domesticum praeconium'), perhaps via Erasmus, *Adagia*, or Fleming (1576: 59).

successful in business, or merely desirous of becoming so. Mr Donald Trump seems named with essentialistic aptness. How different from the Renaissance, when people could be famous for sanctity or virtue. Or is the decline less catastrophic than may appear?

The chivalric world at its best was certainly meritocratic; preferring public service to vainglorious quests, punishing base behaviour, and rewarding virtue with social recognition (as in the Teutonic Table of Honour).[3] In the late Middle Ages a positive thirst for virtue called for the production of countless improving books and paintings of exemplary figures.[4] Nevertheless, historians have learned to look narrowly at the idea of an Age of Faith. Despite official appearances, medieval society was remarkably secular, even—as persisting hero-cults would suggest—incompletely Christianized.[5] As Ernst Robert Curtius shows, the so-called 'chivalric system of the virtues' consisted in the main of secular categories like Germanic 'fealty' and antique *clementia*, with only minor ecclesiastical contributions.[6] Knightly and priestly values might be subtly interwoven; as when authors connected magnanimity and *largesse* with fortitude, or reflected that ancient Temples of Virtue and Honour had but one door.[7] 'Virtue', however, equivocated; to a Federico da Montefeltro, *virtù* would easily have its material sense of prowess, power, strength. Boccaccio's collection of biographies of women, the *De Claris Mulieribus*, is by no means limited to virtuous women. It includes Agrippina, for example, and the prostitute Flora, whose divine fame, indeed, Boccaccio examines reductively. Often the virtues he praises are no better than they should be: in a community valuing lineage, chastity was desirable for practical, secular reasons. Boccaccio pursued wordly glory,

---

[3] Keen (1984: 22, 177, 235); Vale (1977).

[4] e.g. many collections of lives of the virtuous; in visual art, the Nine Worthies and many portrait series. See Hampton (1990), with the review by Reiss (1992).

[5] Keen (1984: 42, 62, 76, 105).

[6] Curtius (1953, excursus 18); cf. Keen (1984: 158–9); Huizinga (1955).

[7] Keen (1984: 55, 158).

yet seems to have felt it a duty to write for posterity—a notable early instance of aspiration to posthumous fame.

Such aspirations did not go unchallenged. The Church had earlier attacked the tournament ethos;[8] now the Church attacked pursuit of fame, calling it 'vainglory'. In the *De Secreto* Petrarch imagines St Augustine accusing him of *superbia* in the form of *honos et gloria* and warning that 'this pursuit of a false immortality of fame may shut for you the way to the true immortality of life'.[9] Petrarch's attitude to fame was somewhat ambivalent; although that did not quite lead him (as William Kerrigan and Gordon Braden argue) to make a dichotomy between suspect contemporary fame and the good fame of posterity. The sequence of Petrarch's *Trionfi*—Love, Chastity, Death, Fame, Time, and Eternity—emphasizes the limitation even of good Fame. After the triumph of Laura and her virtuous company, Death triumphs; after the good Fame of posterity there is a triumph of Time when Fame is forgotten. Petrarch cannot be taken to approve Francis Bacon's attempt 'to cure mortality by fame'.[10] Good fame, too, was a vanity. In visual representations, Time wears a cloak of stars to indicate his comprehensive dominion. At the last he will put it away:

> Shall not I tyme destroye bothe se and lande
> The sonne and mone and the sterres all
> By veray reason thou shalte understande
> At last shall lese theyr course in generall
> On tyme past it vayleth not to call
> Now by this horologe [clock] it dooth well appere
> That my laste name dooth everymore drawe nere?
>
> (Stephen Hawes, *Pastime of Pleasure*, 5635–41)[11]

Yet, against this, there is the Ovidian hope of living in fame, one's better part borne immortal beyond the lofty stars.[12]

---

[8] Keen (1984: 99).

[9] W. Kerrigan and G. Braden (1989: 162); Petrarch (1966).

[10] Bacon (1861: i. 336; 1968).

[11] On Time's stars, see Tervarent (1958, col. 161).

[12] *Metamorphoses* 15. 875–9. Contrast Virgil, *Aeneid* 1. 287: 'famam qui terminet astris'.

The problem of the relation between fame and virtue, already noticed by Cicero, was not resolved by Petrarch in his *De Secreto*: in the late seventeenth century Archbishop Tillotson still thought that to say 'virtue is a sufficient and abundant reward for itself, though it have some truth in it, if we set aside those sufferings and miseries and calamities which virtue is frequently attended with in this life, yet if these be taken in, it is but a very jejune and dry speculation'.[13]

Chaucer's Fame

The vanity of fame is fully envisaged by the father of British scepticism, Geoffrey Chaucer. In his underrated masterpiece *The Hous of Fame* he replaces the brass labyrinth of Ovid's Rumor with a less durable maze of twigs,[14] and equips Fame with what will become her regular attribute, double trumpets. Despite opinion to the contrary, Fame's trumpet was not an ancient motif; although Rumor in the *Aeneid* is assisted by Aeolus and his two trumpets. (The semantic overlap of *fama* and *rumor*, as in *Aeneid* 4. 173–90, was to facilitate many pejorative representations of fame in the Renaissance.[15] The trumpet of Fame probably goes back to St Chrysostom, who makes it a metaphor for vainglory.[16] Subsequent mythographic tradition tells of double trumpets, assigned by Gower to Renomee and Desfame.[17])

[13] Tillotson (1696–1735: iii. 114–15).

[14] *Metamorphoses* 12. 43 ff.; *Hous of Fame*, 1516. The twigs are like those of 'rokes nestes', perhaps alluding to Ovid's *cornix*, changed from white to black for gossiping.

[15] See e.g. Shakespeare, 2 *Henry IV*, prologue; Francis Bacon, 'A Fragment of an Essay on Fame' ('The poets make fame a monster'): Bacon (1878: 519), and *De Sapientia Veterum*, IX: 'querulous fames, and defamatory libels': Bacon (1978: 718–19).

[16] Bennett (1968: 151); see Boitani (1984: 136; also 165 n. 5, 9, on Aeolus as 'windy glory'). Cf. Pride's trumpet in Mantegna's *Seven Deadly Sins*: Tervarent (1958, col. 388). Anciently, the trumpet was an attribute of Calliope, or epic poetry.   [17] Bennett (1968: 153): cit. Boitani (1984: 165 n. 12).

Chaucer's Fame, though tiny, extends like Virgil's Rumor to the sky: 'with hir hed she touchëd hevene, | Ther as shynen sterres sevene' (lines 1375–6). When she wishes to dispense reputations, she calls for Eolus (Aeolus) and his two 'clariouns'. The latter are identified as the golden 'Clere Laude' ('Illustrious Praise', line 1575) and the 'blake trumpe of bras', 'Sklaundre lyght' ('Casual Slander', lines 1625, 1637), which stinks like the pit of hell. So begins the elaborate Renaissance iconography of Fame, with its oppositions of trumpets short and long, good and evil, present and posthumous, anterior and posterior.[18] This last—'Fame's posterior trumpet' (*Dunciad*, IV. 71)—will from the seventeenth century onwards release the deflating farts of countless political satires.[19] A central theme of this iconographic tradition is the doubleness, fickleness, emptiness, or flatus of Fame. Was not Aeolus the god of wind? It might be thought that good Fame, on the contrary, could not be too loud. Yet the tradition attains a fine apotheosis in Prince Eugene's modest muting of Fame's trumpet in Balthasar Permoser's Vienna tableau (1718–21).[20]

Chaucer is well aware of the powerfulness of fame. He insistently identifies chivalric ambition with its trumpets:

> hem that maken blody soun
> In trumpe, beme [bugle], and claryoun;
> For in fight and blod-shedynge
> Ys usèd gladly clarionynge.
> There herde I trumpen Messenus,
> Of whom that speketh Virgilius.
> There herde I trumpe Joab also,

[18] Examples in visual art are legion: for examples from print-makers at Rudolf II's court, see Campbell (1991, nos. 8, 11, 15, 19: Aegidius Sadeler, Bartolomeus Spranger, Hendrik Goltzius, Jacob Matham). For examples in frontispieces, see Butsch (1969: 162–3, 177, 180, etc.).

[19] Schama (1987); Tervarent (1958, cols. 387–8, 'Trompette Romaine'). Cf. Pope's 'black trumpet': *Epilogue to the Satires* (1738), dialogue 1, line 159. A typical example is Hollar's frontispiece to *The History of the Royal Society*: illus. Graham Parry (1980: 107).

[20] *Apotheosis of Prince Eugene*, now in the Lower Belvedere. Cf. Donner's sculpture of Charles VI crowned with the serpent of eternity.

> Theodamas, and other mo;
> And alle that used clarion
> In Cataloigne and Aragon,
> That in her tyme famous were
> To lerne, saugh I trumpe there.
>
> (*Hous of Fame*, III. 1239–54)[21]

The stellification of Fame, as we have seen, could be highly élitist. According to one view, only the famous became stars at death: ordinary mortals turned to clay. On Cicero's more liberal, if somewhat appalling, view, however, 'nearly the whole heaven is filled with mankind'.[22] Chaucer's vision is similar: he abandons his catalogue of martial names because they are 'Moo than sterres ben in hevene'.

A widespread belief survived in folklore that everyone had a star ('dazzling if his lot be brilliant, pale if his state of life be humble').[23] In a version favouring intellectuals, astronomers desired to learn about the stars because they hoped 'to go after . . . death to the places suited to virtue'.[24] Plato might have agreed with that. But in late antique Neoplatonism aspiration was competitive, even after death. Perfected souls went from the Gate of Gods by the Milky Way to join God in the infinite light beyond the stars, but others remained, according to their spiritual degree, in the spheres.[25] Similar grades of spirituality were incorporated into medieval orthodoxy, but disliked for their sacerdotal associations by the Protestant Reformers. It is no accident that Spenser portrays proud Lucifera in a coach

> Adornèd all with gold, and girlonds gay,
> That seemd as fresh as Flora in her prime
> And strove to match, in royall rich array,
> Great Junoes golden chaire, the which they say

---

[21] Cf. III. 1572–82.

[22] *Tusculanae Disputationes*, I. 12. 28. See Cumont (1922: 105).

[23] Cumont (1922: 92).

[24] Philip of Opus; originally a 'Chaldean' view, according to Cumont (1922: 208).   [25] Cumont (1922: 108, 152–3).

> The Gods stand gazing on, when she does ride
> To Joves high house through heavens bras-praved way.
>
> (*The Faerie Queene*, I. iv. 17)

That brazen way is the *via sublimis*, the Milky Way by which the gods fare to the *regalem . . . domum* of Jupiter.[26]

Medieval stellification was inextricably involved with chivalric hero-cults. A poet like John Lydgate—not incapable of piety—could happily write of King Arthur, 'the sun' of Britain, as translated

> Up to the riche sterri briht dongoun—
> Astronomeeres well reherse kunne—
> Callid Arthuris constellacioun,
> Wher he sit crownid in the hevenly mancioun
> Amyd the paleis of stonis cristallyne,
> Told among Cristen first of the worthi nyne.
>
> (*The Fall of Princes*, VIII. 4003–8)[27]

First of the Nine Worthies—those most famous heroes of Christendom—Arthur the Bear of Britain is thus identified with Ursa Major, the Great Bear, Chaucer's 'sterres sevene', the stars also designated as Arthur's chariot. To the Reformers, such a cult was anathema. Stellification or 'translation in heaven' seemed to William Harrison 'a toy much like to the catalogue of Romish saints (although the one was written in the celestial or immaterial orbs, the other in sheeps' skins, and very brickle paper)'.[28] Significantly, however, he concedes fame's value as an incentive. Stellification was 'so esteemed, that every prince would oft hazard . . . the uttermost adventures, thereby to win such fame in his life, that after his death he might by merit have such place in heaven, among the shining stars'.[29] Harrison might not have objected in the same way if the Catholic pantheon had been replaced by

---

[26] Ovid, *Metam.* I. 168–72. Milton is more positive about the Milky Way at *Paradise Lost* VII. 576 ff.

[27] Cf. Gavin Douglas, *Eneados*, III. viii. 21, where Arcturus is 'Arthuris hufe' (i.e. houf, home). See Rathborne (1937: 183).

[28] Harrison (1807: 38).   [29] Harrison (1807: 30); see Rathborne (1937: 3).

one more like Théodore de Bèze's Protestant *Icones*. In matters
of fame, Christianity and chivalry coexisted precariously:[30]
one recalls Federico's Studiolo, with its exemplary portraits,
and below the exactly complementary twin cubicles, the
Cappella del Perdono and the Tempietto delle Muse,[31] and
Achille Bocchi's *palazzo*, with its twin epigraphs, from Horace
and the Hebrew Psalms.[32]

Panthea

The coexistence of fame and salvation is encapsulated within
a mysterious image in *The Faerie Queene*: Panthea, a 'bright
towre all built of christall cleene' which seems to Redcrosse
'the brightest thing, that was'. It is his loftiest ideal—until he
attains a vision from the Mount of Contemplation. Then 'this
great Citie' Cleopolis ('Glory City') with its crystal Panthea is
far surpassed by Contemplation: 'this bright Angels towre
quite dims that towre of glas' (I. x. 58). Cleopolis has plausibly been associated with London or Westminster, and
Panthea with Westminster Abbey,[33] which was known
throughout Europe as a shrine of the great, and where
emblems of fame much like Redcrosse's and Arthur's shields
actually hung.[34] But Panthea also relates to marvels of ancient
Rome: the Holovitreum, the Capitol, and the Pantheon.[35]

These potent symbols of imperial power figured among the
Seven Wonders of the medieval world, described for travellers
in works like the twelfth-century guidebook *Mirabilia Urbis
Romae*.[36] Here, the Capitol is described as a 'mirror' of
power, a marvell 'to all nations', the Holovitreum (glass

---

[30] Keen (1984); Curtius (1953).   [31] Cheles (1986: 13, 36); Wendorf (1990).
[32] Watson (1993: 149).

[33] Other suggestions include Westminster Abbey (A. C. Hamilton), Windsor
Castle (Warton), and Richmond or 'Shene', bright (Queckett): Spenser (1977:
141).   [34] Rathborne (1937: 47).
[35] Rathborne (1937: 118).

[36] Rathborne (1937: 40); Scherer (1955: 4); Nichols (1986).

universe) a sort of planetarium, 'made of glass and gold by mathematical craft, as containing an astrograph with all the signs of the heavens'.[37] Lydgate laments the Holovitreum (destroyed by St Sebastian) as a chief glory of Rome:

> Where is thy temple of christal bright shewing,
> Made half of gold, most richely moustrying [showing]
> The heavenly spheres, by compasse wrought and line,
> Which that long processe hath brought unto ruine?
>
> (*The Fall of Princes*, II. 4484–7)[38]

Such traditions inform one of Spenser's earliest works, an imitation of Du Bellay's strange visions of the ruins of Rome. The marvellous vestiges seem to capture the young Spenser's imagination as they do Shakespeare's—a 'great temple' and 'a stately frame':

> On high hills top I saw a stately frame,
> An hundred cubits high by just assize,
> With hundreth pillours fronting faire the same,
> All wrought with Diamond after Dorick wize:
>   Nor brick, nor marble was the wall in view,
> But shining Christall, which from top to base
> Out of her womb a thousand rayons threw,
> An hundred steps of Afrike golds enchase . . .
>
> ('The Visions of Bellay', stanzas i and ii)[39]

The Mirabilian Capitol and Holovitreum are later remembered when Guyon, reading the Elfin chronicle, comes to Elfant 'of most renowmèd fame, | Who all of Christall did Panthea build'.

Spenser would know temples and palaces of glass in literature and romance—in Boiardo and Ariosto; Morgan le Fay's Castle Plaisant; Gavin Douglas's Palace of Honour ('that hevinlie Palice all of cristall cleir'); and *The Hous of Fame*,

[37] Rathborne (1937: 26); Lehmann (1945); E. B. Smith (1971); Nichols (1986: 45). The 'astrograph' may have been a celestial sphere or an astronomical model. For a starry ceiling in the Golden House of Nero, see Suetonius, *Nero* 31.
[38] Cit. Rathborne (1937: 27).
[39] See Rathborne (1937: 35); Hieatt (1983).

where Chaucer in his dream of success is terrified by the prospect of stellification.[40] The shining, glittering house was a prominent literary motif.[41] But such places also existed outside literature, in the 'lantern houses' of Spenser's own time. From Longleat onwards, glass-walled mansions blazing with light were in vogue;[42] expressing aristocratic aspirations, they realized traditional world-images—images, like the Roman Capitol, of far-reaching imperial power. In literature, these images were often highly idealized, as in Spenser's Panthea, or Richard Lovelace's 'light casements where we play'. The ideal visibility of the spiritual élite (based on Matthew 5: 16: 'let your light so shine before men . . . ') also underlies Portia's Belmont: 'How far that little candle throws his beams! | So shines a good deed in a naughty world'—but there without the conspicuous consumption.[43] Implicitly, the lantern houses signified more than brightness; they may even have suggested the owner's hope (or confident assumption) of fame and eventual stellification. Sometimes this suggestion blends easily into Christian immortality. Spenser, however, distinguishes firmly between true and false glory. Challenging the cynicism of his day, he attempts to reformulate a right social aspiration, to imagine the glory of a Christian gentleman. He anticipates Jonson's embattled houses; contrasting the crystal tower of England's true stars with Lucifera's spurious lantern house—just as he contrasts the courtiers' pursuit of Philotime (False Honour) with Guyon's obligation to the Intended, or with Arthur's quest for Gloriana (Heavenly Glory). Such glory is the shadow of virtue: VIRTUTIS UMBRA GLORIA.[44] The neogothic *mise en scène* of crystal houses, far from merely reflecting fashion, challenges revaluation of fame.

Prominent among the metaphorical structures articulating Spenser's poem was an Arthurian mythology of kingship.

[40] *Hous of Fame*, II. 586–7; cf. 1000 ff.   [41] Yoch (1978).
[42] See Girouard (1983: 72, 106–7, 113, 187, 290); cf. Fowler (1975: 120), on Theobalds.   [43] *Merchant of Venice*, V. i. 90–1.
[44] On Achille Bocchi's Symbol xlii, see Watson (1993: 105).

Royal encomium conventionally alluded to the stellified Arthur, as, for example, in the 1501 pageants for the London Entry of Catharine of Aragon and her magnificent spousals with Prince Arthur. These pageants were the first in England to rival the Burgundian festivals in splendour.[45] The programme, possibly by Richard Maryngton, has an intricate iconographical scheme with astronomical motifs drawn from the Book of Job—'canst thou bring forth Ursa Major in his season? or canst thou guide Arcturus with his sons?'[46] Magnificent rhetoric elaborates allegories of St Ursula, the seven stars of Ursa Major, the Seven Virtues, and especially Arthur–Arcturus.[47] *Arturus* and *Arcturus* are conflated; and Arcturus, the brightest star of the constellation Boötes (Bearward, Bearguard, Waggoner, Keeper of the Wain or Cart), is also in the tail of the seven-starred Ursa Major (Chariot of Charlemagne).[48] Thus the stellified Arthur both exalts Henry VII's Celtic Tudor lineage and aspires to be a national avatar of the imperial myth. Spenser's Arthur, similarly, implies an imperial *renovatio* restorating Charlemagne's just *ordo*.

James I disliked militant Protestantism, and had family reasons besides for disliking *The Faerie Queene*. Nevertheless, in the early years of his reign Arthurian symbolism had a distinct vogue. In 1603 Sir John Harington sent James the New Year's gift of a lantern, with epigrams hailing him as 'hope of future ages, | Bright Northern starre'—meaning not only a famous person from Scotland but also, surely, Arcturus the sovereign lodestar.[49] And in 1610 Jonson made Arthurian

---

[45] See Anglo (1963, 1990); Kipling (1977); S. R. Westfall (1990: 39).

[46] Job 9: 9 and 38: 31–2.

[47] For a separate work by Maryngton on similar topics, see Anglo (1963: 84–5); cf. also Gavin Douglas, *Eneados*, III. viii. 21. On the political mythology of Arthur, see Barber (1972).

[48] Arcturus is alpha Boötes; Chaucer refers to the constellation as 'the sterres of Arctour'. Cf. George Chapman's 'Eugenia', a poem much concerned with fame: Chapman (1962: 284). There, however, the 'Asterism of Seven' (line 555) is probably Corona, catalogued as seven stars by Palingenio.

[49] Harington (1930: 287); cf. Marvell's 'By night the northern star their way directs'; see R. H. Allen (1963: 454–5).

mythology the basis of *Prince Henry's Barriers*, an entertainment commissioned, there is reason to think, as an act of policy.[50] Here the Prince, 'discovered as a star above', announces (ominously as it will transpire):

> I, thy Arthur, am
> Translated to a star; and of that frame
> Or constellation that was called of me
> So long before, as showing what I should be,
> Arcturus, once thy king, and now thy star.   (lines 65–70)

Jonson follows *The Faerie Queene* v in giving *renovatio* a reforming modulation:[51] 'The house of chivalry' is ruined which once 'raised the British crown | To be a constellation' (lines 31–8). Jonson's imagery here relies on a compelling visual logic of sidereal geography. The interconnections of Arthur, crown, imperial chariot, and sevenfold virtues depend on the contiguity on the stellar sphere of the constellations Boötes, Corona Borealis, and the Bears. It is not the poetry, but the celestial globe itself, that confers a crown on Arthur–Arcturus, declaring the manifest destiny of the dynasty—and of Prince Arthur.

In a similar vein (if not actually intended for the *Barriers*), Matthew Gwinne's devices for Prince Henry include 'a hemisphere with bright stars' with the motto INTERMINATIS FULGET HONORIBUS (It glitters with unending honours), as well as 'King Arthur's round table' with PRISCUM INSTAURO DECUS (I revive ancient glory).[52]

Nearly thirty years later, Sir Richard Fanshawe celebrated the completion of the *Sovereign of the Seas*, the largest ship of its time, with an epigram that culminates in a similarly imperial stellification. By 1637 neo-Carolingian allusions were appropriate; so that Fanshawe hopes the ship may be

[50] Graham Parry (1981: 74).
[51] As John Peacock persuasively argues: Peacock (1987: 173). On the political mythology of Prince Henry, see Strong (1986); Graham Parry (1981); Williamson (1978).   [52] Strong (1986: 145).

lodged b'a happy storm upon some sphere,
Be launched a sailing constellation there.
And thence (as am'ral [flagship] of the world) hang forth
A brighter star than that which from the north
Lights the benighted seaman through the main;
So Charles his Ship shall quite eclipse his Wain.

('On His Majesty's Great Ship . . . ', lines 105–10)[53]

One constellation eclipsing another should not be seen as a confusion indicating that imperial symbolism has begun to blur into mere aura: 'eclipse' here simply means 'outshine'.

Astraea

Arthurian mythology and translation to Arcturus were denied to encomiasts of Queen Elizabeth, because of her gender. They substituted, therefore, another myth of *renovatio*: namely, the return of Astraea. This Ovidian myth, too, was a stellification. As George Peele, Edmund Spenser, and others developed it, Astraea was a 'righteous Virgin, which of old | Liv'd here on earth, and plenty made abound'; but

Now when the world with sinne gan to abound,
Astraea loathing lenger here to space
Mongst wicked men, in whom no truth she found,
Return'd to heaven, whence she deriv'd her race;
Where she hath now an everlasting place,
Mongst those twelve signes, which nightly we doe see
The heavens bright-shining baudricke to enchace;

---

[53] 'On His Majesty's Great Ship Lying Almost Finished in Woolwich Dock *Anno Dom.* 1637 and Afterwards Called the *Sovereign of the Seas*': Fanshawe (1964: 19); cf. the version in Bodl. MS Firth c. 1: 'But snatched by some high power of Heav'ns bright sphere | Be launched a sailing Constellation there; | Propitious to the wanderers on the Maine, | Whilst Charles's ship is placed by Charles's Wain'. For a full account of the *Sovereign of the Seas*, see Heywood (1990); Evelyn (1955: ii. 30): 'we went to Chatham to see the Sovereign, a monstrous vessel so called, being for burthen, defence and ornament the richest that ever spread cloth before the wind; and especially for this remarkable, that her building cost his majesty the affections of his subjects, who quarreled with him for a trifle (as it was managed by some of his secret enemies, who made this an occasion) refusing to contribute either to their own safety, or his glory'.

And is the Virgin, sixt in her degree,
And next her selfe her righteous ballance hanging bee.

(The Faerie Queene, v. i. 11)

The political cult of Astraea, with its analogues going back to Virgil's and Dante's imperial mysticism, has been studied by E. C. Wilson, Roy Strong, John King, and especially Frances Yates.[54] Even Yates's definitive account, however, does not quite draw out the astronomical complications.

Astraea first gathered imperial significance in Virgil's prophecy of an Augustan *renovatio*—'Iam redit et Virgo, redeunt Saturnia regna' ('Now the Virgin returns, the reign of Saturn returns')—words that were to echo throughout medieval Europe.[55] The identification of Astraea with the constellation Virgo (another stellification myth) is attributed to the ancient astronomer Aratos, who describes Virgo as bearing an ear of corn.[56] In Renaissance depictions, she may hold in one hand an olive branch (as in illustrations to Hyginus and the star-maps of Willem Blaeu), in the other hand ears of corn (Blaeu, Honter, Hood, Dürer) indicating the position of the bright star Spica, alpha Virginis.[57] Alternatively, a caduceus may announce Virgo's astrological role as a domicile of Mercurius. As Virgo spicifera, Astraea attracted a Romano-British harvest-cult, a natural association that underlies Alexander Pope's vision of *renovatio* and peace in *Windsor-Forest*: 'Sacred Peace . . . That Thames's Glory to the Stars shall raise!'[58] All three attributes—olive, corn, caduceus—were easily associated, in political panegyric, with the ideals of peace, plenty, and harmonious concord.

Elizabeth's role as Virgo–Astraea, later reassumed by the Stuart monarchs, appeared in many pageantry programmes and tournament devices.[59] Sometimes it was represented in

[54] Wilson (1966); Strong (1987); King (1989); Yates (1975).
[55] *Eclogues*, 4. 6: see Comparetti (1872); Eliot (1957); Uhlig (1990).
[56] Yates (1975: 30–1).
[57] For Blaeu, Honter, etc. see G. S. Snyder (1984).
[58] Lines 355–6; the harvest theme is resumed in 360–70.
[59] e.g. London 1591, London 1604, Edinburgh 1633; see Withington (1963, index, s.v. *Astraea*).

directly astronomical terms. For the 1633 Edinburgh Entry, an arch was constructed whose face 'represented a heaven, into the which appeared his Majesty's ascendant Virgo. She was beautified with six-and-twenty stars, after that order that they are in their constellation, one of them being of the first magnitude, the rest of third and fourth'.[60] Camden mentions a knight who 'in the beginning of her late Majesty's reign . . . upon happy hope conceived, made an half of the Zodiac, with Virgo rising, adding IAM REDIT ET VIRGO'. Another had 'the Star called Spica Virginis' with a scroll inscribed MIHI VITA SPICA VIRGINIS.[61] Such symbolism became so familiar that it was enough to allude by number to the twenty-six stars of Virgo in the Ptolemaic star catalogue. Tournaments with an Astraea theme were so arranged that the knights jousting numbered twenty-six;[62] and Sir John Davies of Hereford's *Hymns of Astraea* (1599) consist of twenty-six poems, each an acrostic of ELISABETHA REGINA.[63] The prominence of the cult number was not diminished by the coincidence that the chain of the Garter insignia happened to have twenty-six links.[64] The Garter badge itself is surrounded with stellar rays; although Ashmole makes a point of explaining the error of supposing that 'the glory or star' issues from the Garter rather than the cross.[65]

Coelum Britannicum

Although many Stuart masques contain astronomical imagery or stellar apotheoses, Carew's *Coelum Britannicum* (1634) claims particular attention here, not only for its substantial literary

[60] Drummond, *The Entertainment of King Charles* (1633; 1913: ii. 125). See Fowler (1964: 199–200).

[61] *Remaines*: Camden (1984: 185, 188). See Yates (1975: 59); Brooks-Davies (1983). [62] As in the 1584 and 1590 tilts; see Fowler (1964: 199 n.).

[63] Davies (1975: 71–86); Yates (1975: 66); Fowler (1964: 198–9, 354–5).

[64] Ashmole (1971, facing page 202).

[65] Ashmole (1971: 216). On the device of the French Ordre des Chevaliers de l'Estoile, see Russell (1985: 26).

qualities but for its programme, which is based on Giordano Bruno's conceit of reform of the pagan heavens in *Lo Spaccio della Bestia Trionfante* (1584). The action of Carew's masque consists of the gradual extinguishing of lights representative of constellations, while the satiric outsider Momus persuades Mercury

> to breathe the Thund'rer's just decree
> 'Gainst this adulterate Sphere, which first I purge
> Of loathsome Monsters, and misshapen forms . . . (lines 291–3)[66]

Their dialogue surveys the morals and politics of the British state, while stellar mythology facilitates shorthand evocations—'vain Ostentation in Cassiope' (line 369)—and neat dispositions, like the proposal to embark the vicious in their own Argo and send them to the plantations in New England (lines 376–84). Mythology can discreetly veil the causes of the sphere's corruption: Jupiter is merely said to have 'retransformed to stars' the earthly beauties his 'raging Queen' had turned to beasts, and thus to have established a degenerate nobility. Fortune has replaced Astraea, so that 'impious men engross | My best rewards' (lines 687–99)—a confession recalling Jonson's complaints about the decline of *vera nobilitas*.[67]

The purging of the sphere corresponds to Charles's programme of reform during the decade of personal rule from 1630 onward. As Martin Butler observes, most critics of the later Stuart masques—including Stephen Orgel, Sir Roy Strong, and Graham Parry—describe them as unreal, and as evading supposed confrontations; whereas in fact the 1630s were characterized rather by an attempt at consensus government.[68] The gap between this intention of the King and the actual behaviour of, for example, the judiciary is hinted at by Carew's spokesman Momus, who implies that Charles is excessively virtuous, his orders 'too strict to be observed long' (line 235). Far from the debate in the masque

---

[66] Carew (1957: 161).   [67] McCanles (1992, *passim*).
[68] M. Butler (1987: 118); Orgel and Strong (1973); Orgel (1975); Graham Parry (1981); W. Kerrigan and G. Braden (1989).

being unresolved or ambiguous, it satirizes everything in sight, including its own form, the project of political idealization, and the legal process of reform itself—a thrust not lacking in boldness, since the audience included 120 lawyers.

When all the sphere has been completely darkened, new constellations are introduced to populate it more acceptably. Charles and Henrietta Maria are duly to take their places 'in the most eminent and conspicuous point' as 'the bright Pole Star of this Hemisphere' and the Consort 'crowned with Ariadne's diadem' (lines 90–7). Next, a mob of lesser stellifications recognizes the need for comprehensive renovation of the social system. Faced with the prospect of becoming 'glorious lights' attired 'with brighter flames', however, the Kingdoms betray reluctance ('We cannot lend | Heaven so much treasure'), doubting whether the 'purer fire' to which Jupiter–Charles is to advance them will compensate them adequately for their financial contributions. Recognizing this concern, Carew qualifies the austerity of stellification in the reformed political sphere. Allowing for the deficient, un-Pythagorean aspiration of modern heroes, he hints that a moderate financial commitment may be enough to ensure fame:

> GENIUS. Jove shall not, to enrich the Sky,
> Beggar the Earth, their Fame shall fly
> From hence alone, and in the Sphere
> Kindle new Stars, whilst they rest here.   (lines 992–5)

In a concluding vision the abstract qualities of government and of a subject's good reputation are represented; 'a troop of fifteen stars' of first magnitude, such as Arthur, St George, Guy of Warwick and Bevis of Hampton 'expressing the stellifying of our British heroes'.[69] Inigo Jones's opening scene symbolizing the ruins of the old chivalry is now succeeded by a 'new and pleasant prospect' (line 1012) of garden architecture. A prospect of Windsor Castle, seat of the revi-

---

[69] Lines 1081–2. Cf. A. P. Herbert's 'atrocious' suggestion, execrated by Walter de la Mare, that the stars should be renamed as Pitt, Keats, Bacon, Morrison, Ella Wheeler Wilcox, etc.

vified Garter Order, opens up—still, however, 'afar off' (line 1084). The symbolic importance of the new Garter chivalry need not be elaborated; it was sufficiently demonstrated by the thorough desecration of the Chapel Royal at Windsor during the Interregnum.

More relevant to our present concern is the number of stellified heroes. Why specially a cadre of *fifteen* stars? Ptolemy's listing of fifteen stars of the first magnitude is a possible reason.[70] But it may well be that the number has a deeper explanation. By a familiar number symbolism, fifteen signified spiritual ascent to the heavens by the mystical journey of virtue.[71] The masquers thus exhibit, by their very number, the aspiration Charles desires for his court. Besides defining candidature for fame, the symbolic number fifteen may also have determined Charles's guest list. As Pietro Bongo notes, the cabbalistic expansion of fifteen (summing the series 1, 2, . . . , 15) is 120—the number of disciples present at Pentecost. Now, Charles invited just 120 lawyers to court for the performance of *Coelum Britannicum*.[72] It would be characteristic both of Charles and of the masque form itself that the lawyers should be persuaded to participate in reform by subjecting them to the Neoplatonic magic of the number. But all this hardly squares with the quality of 'cynicism' sometimes attributed to Carew.

Stellifications of fame like those in *Coelum Britannicum* may be regarded as visually associative metaphors. They no less belonged to structures of belief. Indeed, they can have made little sense apart from aspiration to the celestial sphere. Stellar imagery functioned as a time-honoured panegyric device. But this does not mean that stellification was only rhetoric. As Harrison recognized, it originated in star worship, being all of

[70] Eade (1984: 17).

[71] It was the number of steps to the Temple, and of rungs in Jacob's ladder; see Bongo (1591: 406–8); Bellarmino (1615); H. N. Davies (1970: *a*, *b*).

[72] M. Butler (1987: 134); Orbison (1983: 34): the King favoured the Inns of Court with 'a solemn invitation of one hundred and twenty gentlemen of their company'.

a piece with such other pagan vestiges as the stepping of cosmic labyrinths—'quaint mazes in the wanton green'—in country churchyards.[73] And it continued to have an existential, quasi-religious status, as part of the official religion.[74]

---

[73] Shakespeare, *Midsummer's Night's Dream*, II. i. 99; see Doob (1990: 112–18 and index, s.v. *church labyrinths*).

[74] On the vagueness of 16th-century beliefs, see Thomas (1988). Star worship was widespread in medieval Islam: see Ullman (1972).

4
Obelisks and Pyramids

Historians dispute how much chivalry had declined by the fifteenth century;[1] that it declined is not disputed. Where the earlier Middle Ages had ideal quests and monastic orders of knighthood, the later had extravagant festivals and diplomatic ostentation. The knights 'decayd through pride',[2] until meritocratic idealism gave place to mere parade of lineage. Consciousness of rank extended to the cemetery, where family connections determined the location of a grave.[3] Meanwhile, the reliance of increasingly absolutist monarchies on the fire power of their artillery induced widespread disillusionment. The fountain of honour was muddied. Spenser's attitude is representative in his allegory of Philotime, whose clients

> thought to raise themselves to high degree,
> By riches and unrighteous reward,
> Some by close shouldring, some by flatteree;
> Others through friends, others for base regard;
> And all by wrong wayes for themselves prepard.
> Those that were up themselves, kept others low,
> Those that were low themselves, held others hard,
> Ne suffred them to rise or greater grow,
> But every one did strive his fellow downe to throw.

> (*The Faerie Queene*, II. vii. 47)

Satire of court life was not new with Renaissance humanism; and it would be long before name and rank ceased to

---

[1] Huizinga (1955); Kilgour (1937). Their views are qualified in Keen (1977). On the changing concept of nobility in Italy, see Grendler (1969); P. Burke (1987*a*). [2] Spenser, *Prothalamion*, line 136.
[3] Bossy (1985: 30–1); Llewellyn (1990, 1991).

dominate social behaviour. But already individualism gained confidence. It could point to Petrarch's achievement in the *Vita Solitaria*, to Erasmus' in his powerful attacks on chivalric ideals, and to Montaigne's in his *Essais*.[4]

Montaigne's Scepticism

A more personal conception of fame now arose; an individual afterlife in the stars became a common aspiration. Expensive masses for the dead in chantry chapels had shown the depth of late medieval concern about posthumous state and reputation, while dealing still in kinship or collective terms. After the Reformation, for Protestants dismissing thoughts of purgatory, the concern simplified. They could concentrate on providing for personal reputation after death. The cult of intellectual immortality inculcated by the humanists provided one source of hope; it remained to add a cult of personal, almost physical, continuation. Hope came to be invested in offspring—in one's 'line' or 'increase'—not so much implying family as individual continuation. 'From fairest creatures we desire increase'; 'You do it for increase'. 'Increase' became a charmed word for more than Shakespeare, 'posterity' for more than Jonson. All this has reasonably been ascribed to an ebbing of religion: hope now lay with future generations on earth.[5] But the change had also a simple demographic basis. As sermons on the duty of procreation recognized, mortality rates were critically high. Women's expectation of life in late sixteenth-century England fell to nineteen years: more saints were needed for the present world, let alone the world to come. Attention shifted from doctrines of purgatorial Penance to corporeal Resurrection and the new life. These too had their natural realizations: as Shakespeare's *Sonnets* affirm, one lives again in children—'Yourself again after yourself's decease'.

[4] Duby (1988, chs. 3–5).
[5] W. Kerrigan and G. Braden (1989: 51–2, 228 n. 29).

The normal Renaissance attitude to earthly fame might resemble Petrarch's hope that it would lead to glory ever-lasting.[6] But sceptics were not lacking who questioned whether *gloria* was *virtutis umbra*—whether fame and honour had any necessary connection with virtue. Towards the austerity of absolute disjunction, the honest doubt of Michel de Montaigne (1533–92) went as far as any. Noble actions, he points out, may be performed unnoticed; or else 'a hundred clerks can jot it down whose accounts will not last three days'—'how many valiant men have we seen outliving their reputation?'[7] Virtue had best be its own reward—be considered, stoically, apart from honour and glory. The latter are fortuitous ('What is there more fortuitous than reputation?'[8]), since 'to make deeds seen and known is purely the work of Fortune'. Therefore glory should not be linked with virtue: 'So should we disjoin [virtue] from Fortune.' The disjunction is widened further by Ben Jonson; he believes in the fame he confers, but only because he judges each case afresh on its merits:

> study conscience, more than thou wouldst fame.
> Though both be good, the latter yet is worst,
> And ever is ill got without the first.

> (Epigram XCVIII, 'To Sir Thomas Roe', lines 10–12)[9]

Montaigne rejects Baldassare Castiglione's prudential advice to take risks only while in the public eye; holding instead that 'We are taken by surprise between the hedge and the ditch; we must tempt Fortune by attacking a chicken-coop.'[10] He shares St Augustine's view that the testimony of one's own conscience is the true glory. Carneades is complacent in imagining glory to be desirable 'in the same way that we are attached for their own sake to those who come after us even though we enjoy no knowledge of them'.[11]

---

[6] W. Kerrigan and G. Braden (1989: 20).
[7] Montaigne (1958: 476, 1993: 714).
[8] Montaigne (1993: 706).
[9] Jonson (1975: 54).
[10] Montaigne (1993: 707).
[11] Montaigne (1993: 705).

Montaigne's distrust of glory was soon quite widely shared in the changed society of the Renaissance. Admiration of glory was one thing in the early Middle Ages, when titles derived from chivalric deeds, so that person and name and fame easily coalesced. It was another, now that chivalric society was remote and connections of lineage too weak for the bureaucratic load they bore. Not least in the aftermath of the Reformation, new governing cadres tended to lack any inherited ceremonial validation. Accordingly artists, scholars, and poets were commissioned to supply appropriate myths.[12] A very great deal of Renaissance art and literature, directly or indirectly, casts ruler or patron as *triumphator* in a Triumph of Fame.[13] Portraits especially were multiplied to establish the sitter's fame and perpetuate a glorious likeness after death.[14] The confirming of authority through fame comes out conspicuously in royal portraiture, for example in images of Louis XIV as sun or star.[15] Heroes of the Reformation and Counter-Reformation, similarly, were supported by such multi-media propaganda as Théodore Bèze's *Icones* (1580).[16]

All this encomiastic activity threatened to devalue glory by associating it with human frailty. As if apprehensive of this, indeed, portraits often had on the reverse *memento moris* or *vanitas* still lifes.[17] In dramatic representation, glory was even more at risk, being subject to the judgement of audiences. Since all the world was a stage, even kingship might be in danger of lacking applause—'the Royal Actor born | The Tragic Scaffold might adorn'.[18] Before the Essex rebellion it was thought worth while to hire Shakespeare's company to put on *Richard II* with its scene of a sovereign's deposition.

[12] W. Kerrigan and G. Braden (1989: 16); Braudy (1986: 267 ff., 288 ff. and *passim*).

[13] On the influence of Petrarch's *Trionfi*, see Weisbach (1919); Marle (1931–2); Lorgues-Lapouge (1957).

[14] Braudy (1986: 267, 282); Wendorf (1990).

[15] Braudy (1986: 269–70); Mitford (1966); Macdonald (1984); Fowler (1970a). An artist's 'influence' is so called by analogy with astrological influence.

[16] Braudy (1986: 315).   [17] Ember (1989: 30).

[18] Marvell, 'An Horatian Ode', 53–4; cf. Braudy (1986: 268, 318).

Nobility itself was vulnerable to opinion. Anyone could at will assign a sort of fame:

> Had I a trumpet, and that trumpet Fame's;
> A sheet of marble and a pen of steel,
> I would proclaim and grave some noble names
> So loud and deep, Time should not make them feel
> His scythe or teeth; for they should careless stand,
> Untouched beholding his lost running sand.
>
> (Anon., 'Had I a trumpet', lines 1–6)[19]

Similarly Shakespeare prophesies that 'So long as men can breathe' his sonnet will live and give life; much as Spenser promises his future wife 'My verse your vertues rare shall eternize | And in the heavens wryte your glorious name.'[20]

Terms like 'name', 'fame', 'virtue', 'glory', and 'honour' had all become problematic, and called for sharp discriminations. Medieval poets had been known to oppose good and ill fame, praise and *rumor*, perhaps even chivalric knight and *miles christianus*. Now, the finer distinction between nobility of line and *vera nobilitas*—briefly noticed by Dante in the *Convivio*—was pursued more thoroughly. Ben Jonson made it the systematic basis of his administrations of fame.[21] And a similarly bold distinction lies behind Montaigne's denial that fame has any part in true glory: 'Virtue is a vain and frivolous thing if she draws her commendation from glory.'[22]

Montaigne's separation of virtue from the fame of it depended, as is well known, on a systematic disjunction of *res* and *verba*, things and their names. It is less generally understood that this disjunction was not his innovation, but a traditional Aristotelian doctrine of the Schools, where language and reality were agreed to be independent variables such that the first could be corrected by suitable match-

[19] Anon.: Cutts (1959: 137).
[20] Shakespeare, Sonnet XVIII; Spenser, *Amoretti*, LXXV.
[21] Braudy (1986: 297; cf. 323–4, where 'Jonson's attitude toward public fame' is found 'optimistic or at least hopeful'). See, however, McCanles (1992), bringing out the secret rigour of Jonson's scepticism.
[22] Montaigne (1993: 706).

ing against the second. Indeed, Montaigne begins his essay 'On Glory' with an abbreviated quotation of Aristotle's *De Interpretatione*; denying fame to be part of glory: 'There are names, and there are things. A name is a spoken sound which designates a thing and acts as a sign for it. The name is not part of that thing nor part of its substance: it is a foreign body attached to that thing; it is quite outside it.'[23] If words were parts of the things they named, language would be part of the external universe, and man too might be linked with it, as occultists and the superstitious were prone to believe. Against this 'essentialism' (as it has misleadingly been termed) the orthodox disjunctive view of *res* and *verba* was repeatedly reformulated and refined, by Bacon, Galileo, and many others. So-called essentialism gradually lost support, until by the time of René Descartes (1596–1650), it was largely abandoned. Only a decreasing number of increasingly eccentric occultists now held that words need have natural connections with the things they referred to.[24]

Earlier, however, glory had been so closely connected with its names that confusion was easy for those who were not scholars. Spurious myths of noble origin could be constructed on the basis of mere verbal resemblance (or contrived resemblance); as when the British found reason to boast by tracing their ancestry to Brut.[25] Proper names could be taken to imply properties, as indeed the ambiguity of *nomen* (meaning 'name' as well as 'noun') positively encouraged.[26] Many saints' lives in *The Golden Legend*, for example, begin with onomastic speculations. Some, however, preferred to dwell on how, after the Fall, corruption had impaired the true relation between name and thing, reducing it to the merest vestige. Spenserian wordplays often depend on this idea, and

[23] Montaigne (1993: 702). On the commentary tradition of Aristotle, see Arens (1984); Lohr (1974, 1975).
[24] Craig (1972); also Rorty (1980), exaggerating the contribution of Descartes to this change.
[25] Lyte (1588); Rathborne (1937); Levy (1967); Fussner (1970); Piggott (1976: 40 and *passim*); MacDougal (1982). Cf. Schama (1987: 72).
[26] Ferry (1988); Frye (1976: 3–13); Scholz (1988).

in *Paradise Lost* much turns on the devils' loss of their original, angelic names.[27] Adam and Eve's appropriate naming of the creatures, while ostensibly showing their intellectual reach before the Fall, also relates to contemporary terminological reform and to taxonomic projects like John Ray's and Robert Morison's:[28]

> I named them, as they passed, and understood
> Their nature, with such knowledge God endued
> My sudden apprehension . . .
>
> (*Paradise Lost*, VIII. 352–4)

Mingled with the hope of reconstructing prelapsarian 'sensefull Names',[29] however, may be discerned something like regret for the occultists' world of correspondences (with daimons 'whose powers have a true concent | With planet or with element'), a world Milton himself had earlier dallied with and lost (or renounced), and to which he looked back from a more recently fallen vantage-point.[30]

The integral culture of medieval Latinity broke up comparatively suddenly. Its disintegration—accelerated by the Reformation and by national movements relying on vernaculars—must have resembled a new fall of Babel. In visual art, at any rate, countless representations of the Tower of Babel appeared throughout Europe. And in literature, too, the myth was told and retold, as if to mythicize the growth of competing national languages and the lapse of magical names of power.[31] The seventeenth century dreamed of a new universal language.[32] But it was a dream to be realized, in the event,

[27] Leonard (1990). On Patrizzi's essentialistic conception of Adamic language, see Vickers (1988: 739).

[28] New discoveries and consequent reclassifications transformed botany, from Andreas Caesalpinus (1519–1603), John Ray (1627–1705), Robert Morison (1620–83), and T. P. de Tournefort (1656–1708) to the great Linnaeus—Carl von Linné (1707–78). On linguistic aspects, see Salmon (1972).

[29] Sylvester (1880: i. 80–1).

[30] On the linguistic theories involved in Adam's language, see Fish (1967: 107–30); Salmon (1972); Leonard (1990).

[31] Manganelli (1989: 3); Minkowski (1991).

[32] Jones (1986: 209, 268 n. 14).

through mathematics and computing. The universal language Sir Thomas Urquhart proposes in *Logopandecteision* . . . (1653) is logical and mathematical as much as syntactic and semantic.

So far as natural languages were concerned, authority and unity must at times have seemed to be replaced by uncertainty and ambiguity. *Loci* of sanctity and power were disputed, while the venerable symbolic vocabulary was extended, dispersed, diluted, or applied—as in emblems—to ordinary mundane objects.[33] Apart from the Bible (and that was itself a main object of contention) holy words no longer existed for Protestants who like Milton rejected liturgical worship and thought the mystifying of powerful 'names, | Places and titles' a symptom of depravity.[34] Simultaneously, vows and promises had begun to lose their binding power.[35] Indeed, language itself seemed to lose integrity. Ambiguity, from being described as a fault of rhetoric, had become a valued device that mannerist poets deliberately cultivated. In baroque art, as insidiously, schemes and patterns telescoped within patterns multiplied until how much was meant might become uncertain. Plural meanings, overdeterminations, elusive adumbrations of *je ne sçais quoi*: these could be seen as threatening the univocal certainty attributable to the former age, if not enjoyed by it in historical fact.[36]

The irreversibility of all this should not be exaggerated. In time to come Romantic poets would weave their circles thrice and again rehearse magic words: Tractarians would revive medieval sanctities: and Derridean metaphysicians would fret themselves into *aporia* for lack of an *Académie* to authorize meanings and restore essentialism. The paradox is still hard, that words are not things or ideas, only metaphoric structures

[33] Schama (1987: 489).
[34] *De Doctrina*, II. 4: Yale Prose Milton, vi. 666–83; *Eikonoklastes*, ch. xvi: Yale Prose Milton, iii. 503–8.   [35] Canfield (1989).
[36] On uncertainty of meaning, see Harsdörffer, cit. McFarlane (1986: 7). The deconstructive position was effectively refuted in linguistic terms by Sperber and Wilson (1986), and has recently suffered a number of philosophical refutations: see e.g. Ellis (1989); Burke (1992).

speakers improvise and hearers infer meanings from—but that communication nevertheless works determinately enough within a continuous experiential tradition. (The inferences, though often foreseen and prepared for, are not authorized: authority can no more possess meanings than commercial interests can register as trademarks words in common use.[37])

All the same, Renaissance scepticism was devastating enough. Shakespeare allows it its say in *Troilus and Cressida*, where the Greek 'new men' subvert honour by identifying it with success, while among the Trojans it is Pandarus who brazenly claims 'honour and lordship are my titles' (III. i. 15–16). More directly still, Falstaff deflates honour altogether. Before the battle of Shrewsbury the inglorious knight enquires:

What is honour? A word. What is in that word 'honour'? What is that 'honour'? Air. A trim reckoning! Who hath it? He that died o' Wednesday. Doth he feel it? No. Doth he hear it? No. 'Tis insensible then? Yea, to the dead. But will it not live with the living? No. Why? Detraction will not suffer it. Therefore I'll none of it. Honour is a mere scutcheon.   (1 *Henry IV*, v. i. 131–40)

This textbook position, however, is not Shakespeare's only view of honour, which he refers to more than a thousand times.[38] Hal's opposite view is a main theme of 1 *Henry IV*; and in *All's Well that Ends Well* the *miles gloriosus*, aptly named Parolles, shows honour to be a matter of deeds rather than words or reputation: 'Honours thrive, | When rather from our acts we them derive | Than our foregoers.'[39] The King of France takes Montaigne's scepticism in his stride:

> The mere word's a slave,
> Debauched on every tomb, on every grave
> A lying trophy, and as oft is dumb
> Where dust and damned oblivion is the tomb
> Of honoured bones indeed.   (II. iii. 138–42)

[37] Landau (1989: 298–302).   [38] e.g. Palingenio (1574: 52).
[39] II. iii. 136–8.

These are the words of characters: for the dramatist, scepticism about fame would entail more risk. He was engaged in raising the Tudors' fame and supporting the claims they (like his own Henry V) traced to their 'most famed of famous ancestors'.[40]

These views—inconsistent as they may seem—were conventional enough. Two newer notes, however, may be heard from Shakespeare's doubly sonorous trumpet. One is a persistent linking of fame with death. Henry V is 'too famous to live long'; the Countess of Auvergne hopes to be famous 'As Scythian Tomyris by Cyrus' death'.[41] The other is a certain privacy of honour, going beyond mere disjunction from reputation. First Citizen's criticism of Coriolanus is that 'what he hath done famously, he did to that end' (that is, with the motive of becoming famous).[42] Public honour—even 'dying honour'[43]—may always be suspected of interested motivation; perhaps it is inferior, then, to private self-sacrifice. Like Montaigne, Shakespeare admires the sublimer courage that needs no spectator.[44]

> No grave upon the earth shall clip in it
> A pair so famous. High events as these
> Strike those that make them; and their story is
> No less in pity than his glory which
> Brought them to be lamented.
>
> (*Antony and Cleopatra*, v. ii. 353–7)

Here are juxtaposed two fames that Octavius thinks equal: that of chivalric glory and that of private 'pity'. Antony has sacrificed for Cleopatra 'the honour [that] is sacred'; we may know how much that is from his own affirmation: 'If I lose mine honour, | I lose myself.'[45] He sacrifices nothing less than his own self. This suffices for equality of fame with Octavius,

[40] *Henry V,* II. iv. 92.
[41] I *Henry VI*, I. i. 6; II. iii. 6.
[42] *Coriolanus*, I. i. 34–5.
[43] *Antony and Cleopatra*, IV. ii. 6.
[44] Kuin (1989) asks if Sidney died seeking the public fame recommended by Castiglione.
[45] II. ii. 90; III. iv. 22–3.

however differently their respective piteousness and glory may be judged beyond the grave.

Shakespeare himself is a 'great heir of fame'. His glory is too great to need a 'star y-pointing pyramid'—writes Milton modestly, in the act of supplying one. The dramatist whom Jonson stellifies into the constellation Cygnus needs no monument such as was planned (according to William Browne) for Spenser:

> when mighty Nereus Queen
> (In memory of what was heard and seen)
> Employed a factor (fitted well with store)
> Of richest gems, refinèd Indian ore
> To raise, in honour of his worthy name
> A pyramis, whose head (like wingèd fame)
> Should pierce the clouds, yea seem the stars to kiss,
> And Mausolus great tomb might shrowd in his.[46]

The pyramid Milton probably means—and certainly Browne—would not be the squat modern type, but rather a steep finial-like obelisk, like those fashionable in sepulchres of the time. Notable examples include the tomb of William the Silent at Delft and Hubert le Sueur's fine monument to the Duke of Buckingham in Westminster Abbey, each surmounted by four obelisks.[47] The Pope might erect a few very large obelisks in Rome, but all over Britain churches and houses bristled with countless smaller ones.[48] To Thomas Carew they demonstrate vainglory: he praises Wrest Park because it has no 'pyramids and high | Exalted turrets. But Carew had personal reasons for this, to do with the Greys' impecunious-

---

[46] *Britannia's Pastorals*, II. i. 1016–18: Browne (1893: 226); see Stevens (1989).

[47] Graham Parry (1981: 144); Ariès (1985: 56); Colvin (1991, index, s.v. *pyramid, obelisk*). Significantly, funerary obelisks were rare in antiquity: see Colvin (1991: 341). They were still very common in the 18th century, however: Pope designed one as a monument for his mother. See Mack (1985: 366 and fig. 65).

[48] On obelisks in city planning, see Kostoff (1991: 15, 186 ff., index, s.v. *cosmic city, radial city*, fig. 183); Dibner (1970); Iversen (1968); and others cited in Fowler (1970a: 191). On pyramid shape-poems, see Massin (1970: 182, 186). For other examples of pyramids or obelisks, sometimes associated with trumpets of fame, see Marle (1932: ii. 120, 134, etc.).

ness. A more usual view was John Aubrey's admiration of the 'two noble pyramids' adorning the gate of Sir John Danvers's house.[49]

Pyramid and obelisk were closely identified, the term 'pyramid' (from Greek *pyr*, fire) being applied to both. They had the aspiring shape of flame.[50] Francesco Colonna calls a pyramid 'terrible', associating *terribilità* with the fear of God the destroyer and creator.[51] Fascination with Egyptian religion and monuments, already considerable after Colonna's *Hypnerotomachia* (1498) with its pyramid dedicated *al summo Sole*, became more intense in the seventeenth century.[52] John Greaves gave a detailed account of his survey of the Egyptian pyramids in *Pyramidomographia* (1646), on which Bishop John Wilkins drew in *Mathematical Magic* (1648). John Evelyn went to some trouble in 1645 to send home from Venice a stone with authentic hieroglyphs, having made a drawing of it for Fr. Athanasius Kircher.[53] Kircher devoted much of his life to Egyptology; opening the significance of hieroglyphs, Egyptian mythology, and the pyramids themselves in *Obeliscus Pamphilius* (1650), *Oedipus Aegyptiacus* (1652–4), and *Sphinx Mystagoga* (1676). His striking and much-imitated illustrations of the pyramids show steep, obelisk-like forms.[54] Despite much new information, the pyramids remained shrouded in obscure myths. So mysterious were the hieroglyphic images associated with them that they found explanation in terms of the ancient theology. Egyptian priests were supposed to have learnt them from an ur-obelisk at the gates of Eden.[55]

Speculation about the pyramid's significance followed well-defined paths. Stablest of solids, it emblemized the stable

---

[49] Carew (1957: 87); Aubrey (1972: 374).

[50] Both had funerary connections: see Tervarent (1958, cols. 184, 316).

[51] See Barolsky (1990: 120).

[52] e.g. Marsilio Ficino, Pierio Valeriano (1477–1558), and John Webb (1611–72). See Iversen (1968); and refs. in Fowler (1970*a*: 191 n. 2).

[53] Evelyn (1955: ii. 468).

[54] Merrill (1989, p. xxxvi), from *Sphynx Mystagoga* (Amsterdam, 1676), closely copied in Melton (1681). [55] Gilman (1989: 61).

duration of fame.[56] Even a long temporal duration, however, might be insufficient. Babel fell, after all,

> on whose fruitful fall
> History rears her pyramids more tall
> Than were th'Egyptian (by the life these give
> Th'Egyptian pyramids themselves must live):
> On these she lifts the world; and on their base
> Shows the two terms and limits of Time's race:
> That, the Creation is; the Judgement, this;
> That, the world's morning, this her midnight is.

(Crashaw, 'On the Frontispiece of Isaacson's Chronology Explained', lines 17–24)[57]

Material monuments gave hostages to decay; even brass might be eaten away, as Horace's familiar lines recognize:

> Now have I reared a monument more durable than brass,
> And one that doth the royal scale of pyramids surpass

(*Odes* 3. 30. 1–2)[58]

The fame of his own poetry, he affirms, will outlive that of rulers. By a conventional metaphor the glory and immortality of princes were represented, as in Cesare Ripa's *Iconologia*, by 'a gold-clad figure with an obelisk or pyramid'.[59] An obelisk, whether used as a gnomon or as a winning-post for races, implied time's passage to the end of life. This aspect of the symbol receives elaborate treatment in Cornelius Schut's eloquent *Apotheosis of the Earl of Arundel*.[60]

The obelisk was often surmounted by an orb, as in Inigo Jones's Somerset House Water Gate, aspiring beyond earthly glory to the starry sphere.[61] One recalls Propertius' 'pyramids

[56] Wither (1968: 218). [57] Crashaw (1927: 191).
[58] Trans. W. E. Gladstone: Jourdain (1904: 167); cf. 4. 8. The motif is assimilated to Christianity in Cowley's 'Resurrection', lines 8–11: Cowley (1905: 182–3) cf. Cowley, Ode 1, lines 1–4.
[59] Graham Parry (1981: 98); Ripa (1976: 204, illus. 205).
[60] Graham Parry (1981: 132).
[61] For English examples of the obelisk with sphere, Graham Parry (1981: 161); cf. the emblems by Claude Paradin, Adrianus Junius, Jan van der Noodt, and Geoffrey Whitney, see Moseley (1989, nos. 17, 20, 21, 29).

built skywards'.[62] Or the pyramid might specifically imply the flame of stellification. The anonymous lecturer to the Antiquaries in 1600 explains the sepulchral symbolism in similar terms: 'The high pyramids mounting towards the skies bewray a mind in the deceased, aspiring towards heaven.'[63] Material pyramids might moulder, yet there was hope of stellification:

> the light
> Of this enfranchized flame shall shine so bright
> Amidst our horizon, 'twill seem to be
> The constellation of all poetry.
> Tell me not then, that pyramids disband,
> And drop to dust; that time's ungentle hand
> Has crushed into an indigested mass
> And heap of ruins, obelisks of brass,
> That our perfidious tombs (as loath to say
> We once had life and being too) decay . . .
>
> (Thomas Philipott, 'On the Death of Mr George
> Sandys', lines 23–32)[64]

Besides aspiration to immortality, obelisks sometimes suggested immortalizing sacrifice.[65] That association seems to predominate in Canova's beautiful pyramidal monument to Archduchess Maria Christina (d. 1798) in the Augustiner Kirche in Vienna. The image of a family disappearing through the final door communicates something of the terror originally associated with the pyramid.[66]

A learned article by Janet Levarie Smarr has educed the Neoplatonic ideas underlying the pyramid symbolism of Chapman and other Renaissance poets.[67] Chapman's pyramids surmounted by glass represent the eyes of heaven, the sun and moon, and their projection to the earth. Considered thus as acting downwards, the pyramid symbolizes emanation from the divine. Considered upwards, however, it is the

---

[62] 3. 2. 19: 'Pyramidum sumptu ad sidera ducti.'

[63] Hearne (1771: i. 235); cf. Yale Prose Milton, i. 790: the pyramid 'aspires and sharpens to ambition'.   [64] Philipott (1950: 20).

[65] Hersey (1988: 19–20).   [66] Barolsky (1990: 120, 132).

[67] Smarr (1984).

human eye looking to perfection, as in Cusanus' reversed pyramid.[68] Or it may suggest the ascesis of virtue from the material quadrate of the senses to the One: 'the poet's hope to enter heaven as a star' as in Juan de Boria's emblem SIC ITUR AD ASTRA.[69] These concepts are applied by Smarr to explicate Chapman's poem, or explain frontispiece programmes setting out cosmic order through the symbolism of twin pyramids. They apply equally to fame's stellification.

Heavenly and Earthly Glory

Certainly they underlie the thought of Milton's sonnet 'On Shakespear'. But first, let us discuss his rejection of earthly fame in *Lycidas*:

Fame is the spur that the clear spirit doth raise
(That last infirmity of noble mind)
To scorn delights, and live laborious days;
But the fair guerdon when we hope to find,
And think to burst out into sudden blaze,
Comes the blind Fury with th'abhorrèd shears,
And slits the thin-spun life. But not the praise,
Phoebus replied, and touched my trembling ears;
Fame is no plant that grows on mortal soil,
Nor in the glistering foil
Set off to the world, nor in broad rumour lies,
But lives and spreads aloft by those pure eyes,
And perfect witness of all-judging Jove;
As he pronounces lastly on each deed,
Of so much fame in heaven expect thy meed.   (lines 70–84)

Most follow David Daiches in finding here an unsatisfactorily 'pat, aphoristic' climax. 'What possible consolation', asks J. Martin Evans, 'can Milton be expected to find in the announcement that the prize-giving will take place in heaven?'[70] This smart question leads away from Milton's mean-

---

[68] Smarr (1984: 371, 373).   [69] Smarr (1984: 381).
[70] Danielson (1989: 43).

ing, which may be less pat than critics have supposed. Milton may expect us to recall the discussion of fame in Spenser, his 'sage and serious' master. Spenser's epic Muse Calliope—whose 'golden Trompet of eternitie' could stellify Charlemagne—asks

> who would ever care to doo brave deed,
> Or strive in vertue others to excell,
> If none should yeeld him his deservèd meed,
> Due praise, that is the spur of dooing well?
> For if good were not praisèd more than ill,
> None would choose goodnes of his owne freewill.
>
> Therefore the nurse of vertue I am hight . . .
> And mortall men have powre to deifie:
> Bacchus and Hercules I raisd to heaven,
> And Charlemaine, amongst the Starris seaven.
>
> (*The Teares of the Muses*, lines 451–7, 460–2)

Fame's spur is for Spenser a necessary incentive, and one that leads to the stars. The young Milton may well follow Spenser (and Petrarch before him) in associating fame with heavenly glory. If so, the association is not a simple one. Phoebus pointedly distinguishes between the fame that lies in 'broad rumour' and 'fame in heaven'; between fame in the 'pure eyes' of Jupiter and fame as cynosure of a multitude of eyes— an attribute, iconographically, of earthly fame.[71]

A distinction between fame and glory, as we have seen, was common enough.[72] Already in *Lycidas*, however, Milton theologizes the disjunction; insisting on the 'perfect witness' of

[71] Ripa (1976: 156).
[72] e.g. the devout minor poet Astell, 'Ambition' ('Mean spirited men! that bait at honour, praise, | A wreath of laurel or of bays, | How short's their immortality! | But oh a crown of glory ne'er will die! | This I'm ambitious of, no pains will spare | To have a higher mansion there, | There all are kings') and 'In Emulation of Mr Cowley's Poem Called "The Motto"' ('since fame's trumpet has so short a breath, | Shall we be fond of that which must submit to death?'): Greer *et al.* (1988: 334 and 336–7). See Armbrust (1990). An example in visual art is Christoph Jamnitzer's silver goblets for Gustavus Adolphus (1632), showing a terrestrial globe surmounted by Fame paired with a celestial globe surmounted by Minerva: Conforti and Walton (1988: 110).

Jupiter's fame. As John Peter Rumrich puts it, 'glory equals fame minus the intervening variable of fortune'.[73] Also distinctive is an implied contrast between the chivalric 'guerdon' of public honour and private life's secret honour known only to God.[74] For the humanist Milton of Prolusion VII there is no difficulty in reconciling classical and Christian ideas of fame. Christians are 'above all glory':

to have no thought of glory when we do well is above all glory. The ancients could indeed derive no satisfaction from the empty praise of men, seeing that no joy or knowledge of it could reach them when they were dead and gone. But we may hope for an eternal life, which will never allow the memory of the good deeds we performed on Earth to perish; in which, if we have done well here, we shall ourselves be present to hear our praise; and in which, according to a wise philosophy held by many, those who have lived temperately and devoted all their time to noble arts, and have thus been of service to mankind, will be rewarded by the bestowal of a wisdom matchless and supreme over all others.[75]

Milton here aspires above earthly glory to the Spenserian (and not unhierarchical) magnificence of sharing in God's eternal wisdom 'over all others'.

In *Paradise Regained*, however, the later Milton, embittered against the 'places and titles' and alien honour of monarchic triumphalism, rejects all aspiration to supremacy. He now regards glory as God's 'alone of right',[76] whether to receive or to give in turn to those who glorified him. It is not merely that 'true glory and renown' resides in God's approbation and the applause of angels'.[77] More austerely, Messiah asks

> why should man seek glory? who of his
> Hath nothing, and to whom nothing belongs
> But condemnation, ignominy, and shame?   (III. 134–6)[78]

---

[73] Rumrich (1987: 179–80 n. 5).   [74] Braudy (1986: 355–61).
[75] Yale Prose Milton, i. 302.   [76] *Paradise Regained*, III. 141.
[77] Ibid. III. 60.
[78] This approaches the harshness of Greville, who sees earthly and heavenly fame as directly opposed: Braudy (1986: 310).

Even God does not *pursue* glory:

> Yet so much bounty is in God, such grace
> That who advance his glory, not their own,
> Then he himself to glory will advance.   (III. 142–4)

The change in Milton's attitude to honour may also be related to a long-term social change: the revaluation of private life in the Renaissance.[79] The causes and accompanying factors, were multifarious. Feudal loyalties were destabilized, the force of kinship weakening. In the Church, individual communion replaced the communal sacrifice of the medieval mass, as the enclosed confessional ended public confession. In war, altruistic identification with kin or overlord was superseded by sacrifice for the state—or for particular ideas of it. Armies grew larger and more professional: cavalier gave way to officer and gentleman, peculiar offices of rank to deskilled mechanization.[80] Meanwhile, official ceremonies and custom switched from monarchic to republican and back again, each time weakening communal honour but strengthening the power of the state and individual self-possession alike.

By comparison with the Middle Ages, honour was increasingly in the gift of the state.[81] Recognition came now as much by civil service as by personal service: already *Prothalamion* (1596) stellified not an imperial Arthur, or even a heroic earl, but two Inns of Court lawyers.[82] A new, civil honour was emerging, distinct from *virtù* or individual honour. Virtue could aspire above ordinary earthly glory by sacrificing self to satisfy the expectations of the nation. It was like the medieval social miracle, without Christian motivation. What the community approved, moreover, could be unexpected—inexplicable, even, in terms of older criteria (however reminiscent, at

---

[79] Ariès (1985); W. Kerrigan and G. Braden (1989); Bossy (1985); Duby (1988).
[80] See e.g. Keen (1984: 240).
[81] Schama (1987: 221); Anglo (1990: 108).
[82] Lawyers might suggest orientation towards the Cecil cadre, were it not for Essex's patronage indicating the chivalric; see Anglo (1990: 127).

times, of the public honour of antiquity). Private honour, on the other hand, became more individualized. Dryden's remake of *Antony and Cleopatra*, significantly titled *All for Love*, can openly praise the suicides as great lovers: 'No lovers lived so great, or died so well.'[83] In this, one can gauge how far, for Dryden, moral orientation has become personal and private. With ideals internalized to this degree, people may choose to live (or die) purely for their own approbation.

In the Enlightenment, civil society—for all its ostentatiously non-denominational, secular tone—retained in its codes much Christian content, although this was not always very coherently structured.[84] But it suffered from a fatal deficiency: aims of a very distant character were out of its sphere. Once an immediate objective was achieved (or despaired of), meaning became a profound problem—as it has remained to this day. People are left to wish for some vague meaningfulness as the end of effort. When a British weather record was broken recently, the meteorologist Paul Damari said 'Barbourne will go down in history now and it's great to be a part of that.' It is not easy to grasp how far we have come from Petrarch's vision of fame and greatness.

Petrarch might aspire above collective survival to human uniqueness, and entertain hope of individual immortality through fame. But national societies, when they emerged, recognized no such objectives. Far from working against death or aiming at a community of immortals, they pursued increasingly short-term goals. During the Enlightenment, it is true, social objectives were discussed, if simplistically. But, even then, large goals were treated reductively, or abstracted to the point of vagueness. Earlier aspirations to immortality, when not forgotten altogether, were belittled. Dr Johnson condemned the 'hunger of the imagination' that produced the pyramids.[85] More recently, indeed, utopias have been

[83] Act v, line 519.
[84] On the emergence of civic humanism, see Baron (1989).
[85] *Rasselas*, ch. 32.

projected; but realizing them has involved social engineering so disastrous that the very notion of a millennial society has fallen into disrepute. The need is obvious for some other vision, some basis for coherent aims not obviously inferior to those of chivalric Christendom.

For many, such visionary aims can only be conceived of as finding realization in terms of modern science. But science has been diverted from long-term goals, and has become committed to a world-picture with serious shortcomings. We have looked at some of the ways in which Renaissance science responded to the hopes of an officially Christian community. And we have seen that science was then no enemy to religious aims. Rather, it clarified religion's obscurely expressed purposes; sometimes working them out in disconcertingly litera-listic detail. More recently, science has become immeasurably more powerful. But expectation that it will realize religious hopes has lapsed. Indeed, the present scientific world-picture is one that tends to exclude, or explain away, or simply ignore, religious experience and hopes of resurrection. In consequence, seventeenth-century formulations of a stellar afterlife are commonly regarded as merely figurative, or else as unscientific fantasizing. One might compare the problem presented in our own time by frequent reports of encounters with UFOs and their crews.

Nevertheless, the complex of metaphorical themes we have discussed—stellification, and the obelisks, pyramids, and zodiacs of fame—implied a system of interrelated assumptions then shared by many scientists, and closely related, as we have seen, to astronomical discoveries and developments. The belief in a stellar afterlife may seem too bizarre to have had any practical dimension. We assume that stellification should be given a purely spiritual (or else metaphorical) meaning. But one of the thrusts of early science (since abandoned) was to discover how personal immortality might be achieved in literal, material fact. When Milton envisages, as a goal for mankind, that we should become in 'tract of time . . . as immortal gods' (without specifying exactly how that evolutionary goal is to be achieved) he uses the scientific terms of his time, as much as the pre-scientific New Testament:

> So from the root
> Springs lighter the green stalk, from thence the leaves
> More airy, last the bright consummate flower
> Spirits odorous breathes: flowers and their fruit
> Man's nourishment, by gradual scale sublimed
> To vital spirits aspire, to animal,
> To intellectual, give both life and sense,
> Fancy and understanding, whence the soul
> Reason receives, and reason is her being,
> Discursive, or intuitive . . .
> [T]ime may come when men
> With angels may participate, and find
> No inconvenient diet, nor too light fare:
> And from these corporal nutriments perhaps
> Your bodies may at last turn all to spirit,
> Improved by tract of time, and winged ascend
> Ethereal, as we, or may at choice
> Here or in heavenly paradises dwell . . .
>
> (Milton, *Paradise Lost*, v. 479–500)

In the distant future, when travel to planets and stars is common, and mortality differently conceived, seventeenth-century beliefs in stellification may come to seem natural and reasonable.

References

ABRAHAM, LYNDY (1990). *Marvell and Alchemy*. Aldershot, Scolar Press.

ALBERTI, LEON BATTISTA (1988). *On the Art of Building in Ten Books*. Trans. Joseph Rykwert, Neil Leach, and Robert Tavernor. Cambridge, Mass., MIT Press.

ALLEN, DON CAMERON (1968). *Image and Meaning: Metaphoric Traditions in Renaissance Poetry*. Rev. edn. Baltimore, Johns Hopkins University Press.

ALLEN, MICHAEL J. B. (1984). *The Platonism of Marsilio Ficino: A Study of his* Phaedrus *Commentary, its Sources and Genesis*. Berkeley, University of California Press.

———— (1990). 'Marsilio Ficino, Hermes Trismegistus and the *Corpus Hermeticum*.' In Henry and Hutton (1990: 38–47).

ALLEN, RICHARD H. (1963). *Star Names: Their Lore and Meaning*. Rev. edn. New York, Dover.

ANGLO, SYDNEY (1963). 'The London Pageants for the Reception of Katherine of Aragon: November 1501.' *Journal of the Warburg and Courtauld Institutes*, 26: 53–89.

———— (1969). 'The Evolution of the Early Tudor Disguising, Pageant, and Mask.' *Renaissance Drama*, NS 1: 3–44.

———— ed. (1990). *Chivalry in the Renaissance*. Woodbridge, Boydell.

ANON. (1659). *Cleveland Revived: Poems, Orations, Epistles . . .* London.

ANON. (1920). '*Ovide moralisé*': *Poème du commencement du quatorzième siècle*, ed. C. de Boer. Amsterdam.

ANON. (1947). *Pantagruel's Prognostication* (*c*.1660). Ed. F. P. Wilson. Oxford, Blackwell for the Luttrell Society.

ARENS, HANS (1984). *Aristotle's Theory of Language and its Tradition: Texts from 500 to 1750*. Amsterdam, Benjamins.

ARIÉS, PHILIPPE (1985). *Images of Man and Death*. Trans. Janet Lloyd. Cambridge, Mass., Harvard University Press.

ARMBRUST, CHRYS (1990). 'Humanist Re-presentations of "Glory" and "Magnificence" in Spenser's *Faerie Queene*.' *Renaissance Papers*. 27–44.

ARMSTRONG, LILIAN (1981). *Renaissance Miniature Painters and Classical Imagery.* London, Miller.

ASHMOLE, ELIAS (1966). *His Autobiographical and Historical Notes, his Correspondence, and Other Contemporary Sources Relating to his Life and Work.* Ed. C. H. Josten. 5 vols. Oxford, Clarendon Press.

——— (1971). *The Institution, Laws and Ceremonies of the . . . Order of the Garter.* Facs. London, Muller.

ASTELL, ANN W. (1990). *The Song of Songs in the Middle Ages.* Ithaca, NY, Cornell University Press.

AUBREY, JOHN (1972). *Brief Lives.* Ed. Oliver Lawson Dick. Repr. London, Penguin.

AUERBACH, ERICH (1953). *Mimesis: The Representation of Reality in Western Literature.* Trans. Willard R. Trask. Princeton University Press.

AULT, NORMAN, ed. (1928). *Seventeenth Century Lyrics.* London, Longmans, Green.

BACHRACH, A. G. H. (1962). *Sir Constantine Huygens and Britain 1596–1687: A Pattern of Cultural Exchange.* i: *1596–1619.* Leiden, Thomas Browne Institute.

BACON, FRANCIS (1861–74). *Letters and Life.* Ed. James Spedding. 7 vols. London.

——— (1878). *Works.* Ed. James Spedding, Robert Leslie Ellis, and Douglas Denon Heath. vi: *Literary and Professional Works.* Part 1. London.

——— (1968). *Gesta Grayorum . . .* Ed. Desmond Bland. Liverpool University Press.

BAILEY, DERRICK SHERWIN (1952). *The Mystery of Love and Marriage: A Study in the Theology of Sexual Relation.* London, SCM Press.

BAKER, DEREK, ed. (1977). *Renaissance and Renewal in Church History.* Oxford, Blackwell.

BALL, BRYAN W. (1975). *A Great Expectation: Eschatological Thought in English Protestantism to 1660.* Leiden, Brill.

BARBER, RICHARD (1972). *The Figure of Arthur.* London, Longman.

BAROLSKY, PAUL (1990). *Michelangelo's Nose: A Myth and its Maker.* University Park, Pennsylvania State University Press.

——— (1991). 'Leonardo's Epiphany.' *Source,* 11/1: 18–21.

BARON, HANS (1989). *In Search of Florentine Civic Humanism: Essays on the Transition from Medieval to Modern Thought.* 2 vols. Princeton University Press.

BARTON, ANNE (Anne Righter) (1967). *Shakespeare and the Idea of the Play.* Rev. edn. London, Penguin.

BASILIUS VALENTINUS (1660). *The Triumphant Chariot of Antimony . . .* (Leipzig, 1604). Trans. I. H. Oxon (John Harding). London.

——— (1893). *The Triumphal Chariot of Antimony . . . with the Commentary of Theodore Kerckringius* (1685). Trans. A. E. Waite. London.

——— (1962). *The Triumphant Chariot of Antimony . . .* (1685). Repr. London, Stuart.

BATE, JONATHAN (1989). 'Ovid and the Mature Tragedies: Metamorphosis in *Othello* and *King Lear.*' *Shakespeare Studies*, 41: 133–44.

BAXTER, RICHARD (1985). *The Autobiography of Richard Baxter.* Ed. N. H. Keeble. London, Dent.

BEEDOME, THOMAS (1928). *Select Poems Divine and Human.* Ed. Francis Meynell. London, Nonesuch Press.

BELLARMINO, ROBERTO FRANCESCO ROMOLO (Saint Robert) (1615). *De Ascensione Mentis in Deum per Scalas Rerum Creatarum . . .* Antwerp.

BENESCH, OTTO (1965). *The Art of the Renaissance in Northern Europe.* Rev. edn. London, Phaidon.

BENJAMIN, A. E., CANTOR, GEOFFREY N., and CHRISTIE, JOHN R., eds. (1987). *The Figural and the Literal: Problems of Language in the History of Science and Philosophy 1630–1800.* Manchester University Press.

BENNETT, J. A. W. (1968). *Chaucer's* Book of Fame. Oxford, Clarendon Press.

BERGER, ROBERT W. (1993). *The Palace of the Sun: The Louvre of Louis XIV.* University Park, Pennsylvania State University Press.

BERSUIRE, PIERRE (Petrus Berchorius) (1511). *Metamorphosis Ovidiana Moraliter Explanata.* Paris.

BESSARD, BELLA (1990). 'From the City of Man to the City of God.' *FMR*, No. 42: 118–28.

BEVAN, JONQUIL (1989). 'Izaak Walton's Collections for Fulman's Life of John Hales: The Walker Part.' *Bodleian Library Record*, 13: 160–71.

BIADENE, SUSANNA, ed. (1990). *Titian.* Exhibition Catalogue. Venice, Marsilio Editori.

BIENKOWSKA, BARBARA, ed. (1973). *The Scientific World of Copernicus on the Occasion of the 500th Anniversary of his Birth 1473–1973.* Dordrecht, Reidel.

BLOUNT, CHARLES (1695). *Miscellaneous Works.* London.

BLUMENBERG, HANS (1987). *The Genesis of the Copernican World.* Trans. Robert M. Wallace. Cambridge, Mass., MIT Press.

BLUNDEN, EDMUND, and MELLOR, B., eds. (1963). *Wayside Poems of the Seventeenth Century.* Hong Kong University Press.

BOEHME, JACOB (1969). The Signature of All Things *and Other Writings.* Repr. London, Dent; New York, Dutton.

BOITANI, PIERO (1984). *Chaucer and the Imaginary World of Fame.* Cambridge, Boydell & Brewer; Totowa, NJ, Barnes & Noble.

BOLGAR, R. R. (1954). *The Classical Heritage and its Beneficiaries.* Cambridge University Press.

BONGO, PIETRO (1591). *Numerorum Mysteria . . .* Bergamo.

BOSSY, JOHN (1985). *Christianity in the West 1400–1700.* Oxford University Press.

BOYD, JOHN D. (1980). *The Function of Mimesis and its Decline.* Rev. edn. New York, Fordham University Press.

BOYLE, M. O'R. (1981). *Christening Pagan Mysteries: Erasmus in Pursuit of Wisdom.* Toronto University Press.

BRAHE, TYCHO (1969). *His Astronomical Conjecture of the New and Much Admired Star which appeared in the Year 1572* (1632). Repr. Amsterdam, Da Capo.

BRANN, NOEL L. (1981). *The Abbot Trithemius (1462–1516): The Renaissance of Monastic Humanism.* Brill, Leiden.

BRAUDEL, FERNAND (1981). *The Structures of Everyday Life.* Trans. Siân Reynolds. London, Collins; New York, Harper & Row.

BRAUDY, LEO (1986). *The Frenzy of Renown: Fame and its History.* New York, Oxford University Press.

BRAUNMULLER, A. R. (1973), 'The Serious Comedy of Greene's *James IV*', *English Literary Renaissance* 3: 335–50.

BRETT, ARTHUR (1660). *Threnodia, Or the Death of the Duke of Gloucester.* Oxford.

BROCKLISS, L. W. B. (1690). 'Copernicus in the University: The French Experience.' In Henry and Hutton (1990: 190–213).

BRODERICK, HERBERT R. (1982). 'Some Attitudes toward the Frame in Anglo-Saxon Manuscripts of the Tenth and Eleventh Centuries.' *Artibus et Historiae,* 5: 31–42.

B[ROME], R[ICHARD], ed. (1649). *Lachrymae Musarum: The Tears of the Muses, Expressed in Elegies.* London.

BROOKE, JOHN HEDLEY (1991). *Science and Religion: Some Historical Perspectives.* Cambridge University Press.

BROOKS-DAVIES, DOUGLAS (1983). *The Mercurian Monarch: Magical Politics from Spenser to Pope.* Manchester University Press.

———— (1988). ' "Thoughts of Gods": Messianic Alchemy in *Windsor-Forest.*' *Yearbook of English Studies,* 18: 125–42.

BROWNE, WILLIAM (1893). *Poems of William Browne of Tavistock.* Ed. Gordon Goodwin. 2 vols. London.

BULLEN, J. B. (1994). *The Myth of the Renaissance in Nineteenth-Century Writing.* Oxford, Clarendon Press.

BURCKHARDT, JACOB (1985). *The Architecture of the Italian Renaissance.* Trans. Peter Murray. Repr. London, Secker & Warburg.

BURKE, PETER (1987a). *The Italian Renaissance: Culture and Society in Italy* (1972). Rev. edn. Princeton University Press.

———— (1987b). *The Renaissance.* London, Macmillan.

———— (1992). *The Fabrication of Louis XIV.* New Haven, Yale University Press.

BURKE, SEÁN (1992). *The Death and Return of the Author: Criticism and Subjectivity in Barthes, Foucault and Derrida.* Edinburgh University Press.

BURKERT, WALTER (1973). *Lore and Science in Ancient Pythagoreanism.* Trans. E. L. Minar. Cambridge, Mass., Harvard University Press.

BURNS, NORMAN T. (1972). *Christian Mortalism from Tyndale to Milton.* Cambridge, Mass., Harvard University Press.

BURROUGHS, CHARLES (1990). *From Signs to Design: Environmental Process and Reform in Early Renaissance Rome.* Cambridge, Mass., MIT Press.

BURTON, ROBERT (1989–). *The Anatomy of Melancholy.* Ed. J. B. Bamborough, Rhonda L. Blair, Thomas C. Faulkner, and Nicolas K. Kiessling. Oxford, Clarendon Press.

BUSH, DOUGLAS (1961). 'Science and Literature.' In Toulmin *et al.* (1961: 29–62).

BUTLER, I. CHRISTOPHER (1970). *Number Symbolism.* London, Routledge & Kegan Paul.

BUTLER, MARTIN (1987). 'Politics and the Masque: *The Triumph of Peace.*' *The Seventeenth Century,* 2: 117–41.

BUTSCH, ALBERT FIDELIS (1969). *Handbook of Renaissance Ornament.* Rev. Alfred Werner. New York, Dover.

CALDERWOOD, JAMES L. (1987). *Shakespeare and the Denial of Death.* Amherst, University of Massachusetts Press.

CALVIN, JEAN (1949). *Institutes of the Christian Religion.* Trans. Henry Beveridge. 2 vols. Repr. London, Clarke.

The Cambridge History of Renaissance Philosophy (1988). Gen. ed. Charles B. Schmitt. Ed. Quentin Skinner, Eckhard Kessler, and Jill Kraye. Cambridge University Press.

CAMDEN, WILLIAM (1984). *Remains Concerning Britain.* Ed. R. D. Dunn. University of Toronto Press.

CAMILLE, MICHAEL (1992). *Image on the Edge: The Margins of Medieval Art.* London, Reaktion.

CAMPBELL, MUNGO (1991). *The Stylish Image: Printmakers in the Court of Rudolf II.* Exhibition Catalogue. Edinburgh, National Gallery of Scotland.

CANFIELD, J. DOUGLAS (1989). *Word as Bond in English Literature from the Middle Ages to the Restoration.* Philadelphia, University of Pennsylvania Press.

CAREW, THOMAS (1957). *The Poems of Thomas Carew with his Masque Coelum Britannicum.* Ed. Rhodes Dunlap. Rev. edn. Oxford, Clarendon Press.

CARRUTHERS, MARY (1990). *The Book of Memory: A Study of Memory in Medieval Culture.* Cambridge University Press.

CATS, JACOB (1632). *Spiegel van den Ouden ende Nieuwen Tijdt . . .* The Hague.

CAXTON, WILLIAM (1913). *Mirrour of the World.* Ed. Oliver H. Prior. London, Paul, Trench & Trübner; Oxford University Press for the Early English Text Society.

CESAREO, FRANCESCO CIRIACO (1990). *Humanism and Catholic Reform: The Life and Work of Gregorio Cortese (1483–1548).* Renaissance and Baroque: Studies and Texts, 11. New York, Lang.

CHAMBERS, A. B. (1992). *Transfigured Rites in Seventeenth-Century English Poetry.* Columbia, Missouri University Press.

CHAPMAN, GEORGE (1962). *The Poems of George Chapman.* Ed. Phyllis Brooks Bartlett. Repr. New York, Russell & Russell.

CHARTIER, ROGER, ed. (1989). *A History of Private Life*: ii: *Revelations of the Medieval World.* Gen. eds. Philippe Ariès and Georges Duby. Trans. Arthur Goldhammer. Cambridge, Mass., Harvard University Press/Belknap.

CHELES, LUCIANO (1986). *The Studiolo of Urbino: An Iconographic Investigation.* University Park, Pennsylvania State University Press.

CLARK, JONATHAN C. D. (1986). *Revolution and Rebellion: State and*

Society in England in the Seventeenth and Eighteenth Centuries. Cambridge University Press.

CLARKSON, LESLIE (1976). *Death, Disease, and Famine in Pre-Industrial England.* New York, St Martin's.

COHEN, I. BERNARD, DUFFIN, K. E., and STRICKLAND, STUART (1990). *Puritanism and the Rise of Modern Science: The Merton Thesis.* New Brunswick, NJ, Rutgers University Press; London, Eurospan.

COLIE, ROSALIE L. (1973). *The Resources of Kind: Genre-Theory in the Renaissance.* Ed. Barbara Kiefer Lewalski. Berkeley, University of California Press.

COLLINS, STEPHEN L. (1989). *From Divine Cosmos to Sovereign State: An Intellectual History of Consciousness and the Idea of Order in Renaissance England.* Oxford University Press.

COLLOP, JOHN (1962). *Poems.* Ed. Conrad Hilberry. Madison, University of Wisconsin Press.

COLVIN, HOWARD (1991). *Architecture and the After-Life.* New Haven, Yale University Press.

COMPARETTI, DOMENICO (1872). *Vergilio nel Medioevo.* Livorno.

CONFORTI, MICHAEL, and WALTON, GUY, eds. (1988). *Royal Treasures of Sweden 1550–1700.* Exhibition Catalogue. University of Chicago for National Gallery of Art, Washington.

CONRAD, JOSEPH (1946). *Youth; Heart of Darkness; The End of the Tether.* Coll. edn. London, Dent.

COPENHAVER. See *Hermetica.*

COWLEY, ABRAHAM (1668). *Poemata Latina.* London.

——— (1905). *Poems: Miscellanies, The Mistress, Pindarique Odes, Davideis, Verses Written on Several Occasions.* Ed. A. R. Waller. Cambridge University Press.

COX, JOHN D. (1989). *Shakespeare and the Dramaturgy of Power.* Princeton University Press.

COYNE, G. V., HELLER, M., and ZYCIŃSKI, J., eds. (1985). *The Galileo Affair, A Meeting of Faith and Science: Proceedings of the Cracow Conference . . . 1984.* Vatican, Specola Vaticana.

CRAIG, MARTHA (1972). 'The Secret Wit of Spenser's Language.' In A. C. Hamilton, ed., *Essential Articles for the Study of Edmund Spenser.* Hamden, Conn., Archon.

CRASHAW, RICHARD (1927). *The Poems English, Latin and Greek of Richard Crawshaw.* Ed. L. C. Martin. Rev. edn. Oxford, Clarendon Press.

CROMBIE, A. C. (1961). *Augustine to Galileo.* 2 vols. Rev. edn. London, Heinemann.

CUMONT, FRANZ (1922). *After Life in Roman Paganism.* Silliman Lectures. New Haven, Yale University Press.

CURTIUS, ERNST ROBERT (1953). *European Literature and the Latin Middle Ages* (1948). Trans. Willard R. Trask. London, Routledge.

CUTTS, JOHN P. (1959). *Seventeenth Century Songs and Lyrics.* Columbia, University of Missouri Press.

DALES, RICHARD C. (1980). 'The De-animation of the Heavens in the Middle Ages.' *Journal of the History of Ideas,* 41: 531–50.

———— (1990). *Medieval Discussions of the Eternity of the World.* Leiden, Brill.

DALY, PETER M., ed. (1988). *The English Emblem and Continental Tradition.* New York, AMS.

D'AMICO, J. F. (1983). *Renaissance Humanism in Papal Rome.* Baltimore, Johns Hopkins University Press.

DANIEL, GEORGE (1878). *The Poems of George Daniel.* Ed. A. B. Grosart. 4 vols. Boston.

———— (1959). *The Selected Poems of George Daniel of Beswick 1616–1657.* Ed. Thomas B. Stroup. Lexington, University of Kentucky Press.

DANIELSON, DENNIS (1989). *The Cambridge Companion to Milton.* Cambridge University Press.

DAVENANT, SIR WILLIAM (1972). *The Shorter Poems and Songs from the Plays and Masques.* Ed. A. M. Gibbs. Oxford, Clarendon Press.

DAVIES, H. NEVILLE (1970a). 'The Structure of Dryden's *A Song for St Cecilia's Day, 1690.*' In Fowler (1970b: 201–33).

———— (1970b). 'The First English Translations of Bellarmine's *De Ascensione Mentis.*' *Library,* 25: 49–52.

DAVIES, SIR JOHN (1975). *The Poems of Sir John Davies.* Ed. Robert Krueger. Oxford, Clarendon Press.

DEAR, PETER ROBERT (1990). *Mersenne and the Learning of the Schools.* Ithaca, NY, Cornell University Press.

DEBUS, ALLEN G. (1970). *Science and Education in the Seventeenth Century: The Webster–Ward Debate.* London, Macdonald; New York, American Elsevier.

DELUMEAU, JEAN (1991). *Sin and Fear: The Emergence of a Western Guilt Culture: Thirteenth–Eighteenth Centuries.* Trans. Eric Nicholson. Manchester University Press.

DEMARAY, JOHN G. (1990). *Cosmos and Epic Representation: Dante,*

Spenser, Milton and the Transformation of Renaissance Heroic Poetry. Pittsburgh, Penn.: Duquesne University Press.

DENHAM, SIR JOHN (1969). *The Poetical Works.* Ed. Theodore Howard Banks. Hamden, Conn.: Archon.

DIBNER, BERN (1970). *Moving the Obelisks . . .* Cambridge, Mass., MIT Press.

DICKENS, CHARLES (1986). *Barnaby Rudge.* Ed. Gordon Spence. London, Penguin.

DIJKSTERHUIS, E. J. (1986). *The Mechanization of the World Picture* (1950). Trans. C. Dikshoorn. Princeton University Press.

DOBBS, BETTY JO TEETER (1991). *The Janus Faces of Genius: The Role of Alchemy in Newton's Thought.* Cambridge University Press.

DOLLERUP, CAY (1985). 'The Earliest Space Voyages in the Renaissance, Heliocentric Solar System.' In Luk de Vos, ed., *Just the Other Day.* Antwerp, EXA.

DONNE, JOHN (1952). *Essays in Divinity.* Ed. Evelyn M. Simpson Oxford, Clarendon Press.

———— (1965). *The Elegies and the Songs and Sonnets.* Ed. Helen Gardner. Oxford, Clarendon Press.

DOOB, PENELOPE REED (1990). *The Idea of the Labyrinth from Classical Antiquity through the Middle Ages.* Ithaca NY, Cornell University Press.

DRAKE, STILLMAN, trans. and ed. (1957). *Discoveries and Opinions of Galileo.* Garden City, NY, Doubleday.

———— (1970). *Galileo Studies: Personality, Tradition, and Revolution.* Ann Arbor, University of Michigan Press.

DRAYTON, MICHAEL (1931–41). *The Works of Michael Drayton.* Ed. J. William Hebel, Kathleen Tillotson, and Bernard H. Newdigate. 5 vols. Oxford, Shakespeare Head Press.

DREXELIUS, HIEREMIAS (1978). *Zodiacus Christianus* (Munich, 1618 etc.). Facs of Rouen 1633. Ed. D. M. Rogers. Ilkley, Scolar Press.

DREYER, J. L. E. (1953). *A History of Astronomy from Thales to Kepler.* Rev. edn. New York, Dover.

DRUMMOND, WILLIAM (1913). *The Poetical Works of William Drummond of Hawthornden, with* A Cypress Grove. Ed. L. E. Kastner. 2 vols. Edinburgh, Blackwood for the Scottish Text Society.

DRYDEN, JOHN (1958). *The Poems of John Dryden.* Ed. James Kinsley. 4 vols. Oxford, Clarendon Press.

———— (1972). *All for Love.* Ed. David M. Vieth. Lincoln, University of Nebraska Press.

138 REFERENCES

DSB (*Dictionary of Scientific Biography*). Gen. ed. Charles Coulston Gillespie. 16 vols. New York, Scribner's. 1970–80.

DU BARTAS, SIEUR GUILLAUME DE SALLUSTE (1979). *The Divine Weeks and Works of Guillaume de Saluste, Sieur du Bartas*. Trans. Joshua Sylvester. Ed. Susan Snyder. 2 vols. Oxford, Clarendon Press.

DUBY, GEORGES, ed. (1988). Gen. eds. Philippe Ariès and Georges Duby. *A History of Private Life*. ii: *Revelations of the Medieval World*. Trans. Arthur Goldhammer, Cambridge, Mass., Harvard University Press/Belknap.

DUNLOP, ALEXANDER (1970). 'The Unity of Spenser's *Amoretti*.' In Fowler (1970: 153–69).

EADE, J. C. (1984). *The Forgotten Sky: A Guide to Astrology in English Literature*. Oxford, Clarendon Press.

EISENBICHLER, KONRAD, ed. (1991). *Crossing the Boundaries: Christian Piety and the Arts in Italian Medieval Renaissance Confraternities*. Kalamazoo, Medieval Institute, West Michigan University Press.

ELIOT, THOMAS STEARNS (1957). 'Virgil and the Christian World.' In *On Poetry and Poets*. London, Faber & Faber.

ELLIS, JOHN (1989). *Against Deconstruction*. Princeton University Press.

EMBER, ILDIKÓ (1989). *Delights for the Senses: Dutch and Flemish Still-Life Paintings from Budapest*. Seattle, University of Washington Press.

EMERSON, ROGER (1980). 'Sir Robert Sibbald, Kt, the Royal Society of Scotland and the Origins of the Scottish Enlightenment.' *Annals of Science*, 45: 41–72.

ENGLANDER, DAVID, NORMAN, DIANA, O'DAY, ROSEMARY, and OWENS, W. R., eds. (1990). *Culture and Belief in Europe 1450–1600: An Anthology of Sources*. Oxford, Blackwell for the Open University.

ERSKINE-HILL, HOWARD (1983). *The Augustan Idea in English Literature*. London, Arnold.

ERTZ, K. (1984). *Jan Brueghel Der Jüngere (1601–1678)* . . . Freren, Luca.

EVELYN, JOHN (1955). *The Diary* . . . Ed. E. S. de Beer. 6 vols. Oxford, Clarendon Press.

FAGIOLO, MARCELLO (1993). 'A Villa "Tuscan" and Imperial.' *FMR*, No. 64: 100–21.

FANE, MILDMAY, EARL OF WESTMORLAND (1879). *The Poems of*

Mildmay, Second Earl of Westmorland (1648). Ed. Alexander B. Grosart. Blackburn, privately printed.

FANSHAWE, SIR RICHARD (1964). *Shorter Poems and Translations*. Ed. N. W. Bawcutt. Liverpool University Press.

FARMER, NORMAN K. (1984). *Poets and the Visual Arts in Renaissance England*. Austin, University of Texas Press.

FEBVRE, LUCIEN PAUL VICTOR (1982). *The Problem of Unbelief in the Sixteenth Century: The Religion of Rabelais*. Trans. Beatrice Gottlieb. Cambridge, Mass., Harvard University Press.

—————— and MARTIN, HENRI-JEAN (1976). *The Coming of the Book: The Impact of Printing 1450–1800*. Trans. David Gerard. Ed. Geoffrey Nowell-Smith and David Wootton. London, New Left Books.

FEHL, PHILIPP P. (1972). *The Classical Monument: Reflections on the Connection between Morality and Art in Greek and Roman Sculpture*. New York University Press.

FELD, HARTMUT (1990). *Der Ikonoklasmus des Westens*. Leiden, Brill.

FELLOWES. *See* Sternfeld and Greer.

FELPERIN, HOWARD (1977). *Shakespearean Representation: Mimesis and Modernity in Elizabethan Tragedy*. Princeton University Press.

FERRY, ANNE (1975). *All in War with Time: Love Poetry of Shakespeare, Donne, Jonson, Marvell*. Cambridge, Mass., Harvard University Press.

—————— (1988). *The Art of Naming*. Chicago University Press.

FIELD, J. V. (1988). *Kepler's Geometrical Cosmology*. London, Athlone.

FILIPCZAK, ZIRKA ZAREMBA (1987). *Picturing Art in Antwerp 1550–1700*. Princeton University Press.

FINCH, ANNE KINGSMILL, COUNTESS OF WINCHILSEA (1903). *The Poems of Anne, Countess of Winchilsea*. University of Chicago Press.

FINUCANE, R. C. (1981). 'Sacred Corpse, Profane Carrion: Social Ideals and Death Rituals in the Later Middle Ages.' In Joachim Whaley, ed., *Mirrors of Mortality: Studies in the Social History of Death*. New York, St Martin's Press.

FISH, STANLEY (1967). *Surprised by Sin*. Berkeley, University of California Press.

FIXLER, MICHAEL (1964). *Milton and the Kingdoms of God*. London, Faber.

FLEMING, ABRAHAM (1576). *A Panoply of Epistles . . . .* London.

FLETCHER, GILES (1964). *The English Works of Giles Fletcher, the Elder*. Madison, University of Wisconsin Press.

FLINT, VALERIE I. J. (1991). *The Rise of Magic in Early Medieval Europe.* Oxford, Clarendon Press.

FONTENELLE, BERNARD LE BOVIER DE (1695). *A Plurality of Worlds.* Trans. John Glanvill. London.

———— (1955). *Entretiens sur la pluralité des mondes . . .* (1686). Ed. Robert Shackleton. Oxford, Clarendon Press.

———— (1990). *Conversations on the Plurality of Worlds* (1686). Trans. H. A. Hargreaves. Berkeley, University of California Press.

FOWLER, ALASTAIR (1964). *Spenser and the Numbers of Time.* London, Routledge; New York, Barnes & Noble.

———— (1970a). *Triumphal Forms: Structural Patterns in Elizabethan Poetry.* Cambridge University Press.

———— (1970b). *Silent Poetry: Essays in Numerological Analysis.* London, Routledge.

———— (1975). *Conceitful Thought: The Interpretation of English Renaissance Poems.* Edinburgh University Press.

———— (1980). 'Robert Herrick.' Warton Lecture. *Proceedings of the British Academy,* 66: 243–64.

———— (1987). 'The Plays within the Play in *Hamlet.*' In John W. Mahon and Thomas A. Pendleton, eds., *'Fanned and Winnowed Opinions': Shakespearean Essays Presented to Harold Jenkins.* London, Methuen.

———— (1991). *The New Oxford Book of Seventeenth Century Verse.* Oxford University Press.

———— (1994). *The Country House Poem: A Cabinet of Seventeenth-Century Estate Poems and Related Items.* Edinburgh University Press.

———— (1995). ' "Cut without Hands": Herbert's Christian Altar.' In Howard Erskine-Hill and Richard McCabe, eds., *Presenting Poetry.* Cambridge University Press.

FRECCERO, JOHN (1968). 'The Dance of the Stars: *Paradiso* X.' *Dante Studies,* 86: 85–111.

FREEDBERG, DAVID (1981). 'The Origins and Rise of the Flemish Madonna in a Rose Garland.' *Munchener Jahrbuch,* 32: 115.

———— (1988). *Iconoclasm and Painting in the Revolt of the Netherlands.* New York, Garland.

FRYE, NORTHRUP (1976). *Fools of Time: Studies in Shakespearian Tragedy.* Toronto University Press.

FULGENTIUS (1971). *Fulgentius the Mythographer.* Trans. Leslie George Whitbread. Columbus, Ohio State University Press.

FUNKENSTEIN, AMOS (1986). *Theology and the Scientific Imagination from the Middle Ages to the Seventeenth Century.* Princeton University Press.

FUSSNER, F. SMITH (1970). *Tudor History and the Historians.* New York, Basic Books.

GALE, THEOPHILUS (1672). *The Court of the Gentiles; or, A Discourse Touching the Original of Human Literature, both Philology and Philosophy, from the Scriptures.* Oxford.

GATTI, HILARY (1989). *The Renaissance Drama of Knowledge: Giordano Bruno in England.* London, Routledge.

GELLINEK, CHRISTIAN (1983). *Hugo Grotius.* Boston, Twayne.

GILMAN, ERNEST B. (1986). *Iconoclasm and Poetry in the English Reformation: Down Went Dagon.* University of Chicago Press.

———— (1989). 'Word and Image in Quarles' *Emblemes.*' In W. J. T. Mitchell, ed., *The Language of Images.* University of Chicago Press.

GINGERICH, OWEN (1973). 'Copernicus and Tycho.' *Scientific American,* 209: 85–101.

GIROUARD, MARK (1983). *Robert Smythson and the Elizabethan Country House.* Rev. edn. New Haven, Yale University Press.

GOFFMAN, ERVING (1974). *Frame Analysis: An Essay on the Organization of Experience.* Cambridge, Mass.: Harvard University Press.

GRANT, PATRICK (1985). *Literature and the Discovery of Method in the English Renaissance.* London, Macmillan.

GRAZIA, MARGRETA DE (1980). 'The Secularization of Language in the Seventeenth Century.' *Journal of the History of Ideas,* 41: 319–29.

GREENE, THOMAS M. (1982). *The Light in Troy: Imitation and Discovery in Renaissance Poetry.* New Haven, Yale University Press.

GREENWOOD, JOHN PHILIP PETER (1988). *Shifting Perspectives and the Stylish Style: Mannerism in Shakespeare and his Jacobean Contemporaries.* University of Toronto Press.

GREER, GERMAINE, HASTINGS, SUSAN, MEDOFF, JESLYN, and SANSONE, MELINDA, eds. (1988). *Kissing the Rod: An Anthology of Seventeenth-Century Women's Verse.* London, Virago.

GRENDLER, PAUL (1969). *Critics of the Italian World (1530): Anton Francesco Doni, Nicolò Franco and Ortensio Lando.* Madison, University of Wisconsin Press.

GRIMM, CLAUS (1981). *The Book of Picture Frames.* Trans. Nancy M. Gordon and Walter L. Strauss. New York, Abaris.

———— (1989). *Still Life.* Stuttgart, Belser.

GUTHKE, KARL S. (1991). *The Last Frontier: Imagining Other Worlds, from the Copernican Revolution to Modern Science Fiction.* Trans. Helen Atkins. Ithaca, NY, Cornell University Press.

HABINGTON, WILLIAM (1938). *The Poems of William Habington.* Ed. Kenneth Allott. Liverpool University Press.

HAGEN, MARGARET A. (1986). *Varieties of Realism: Geometries of Representational Art.* Cambridge University Press.

HAIGH, CHRISTOPHER (1993). *English Reformations: Religion, Politics and Society under the Tudors.* Oxford, Clarendon Press.

HALL, BASIL (1990). *Humanists and Protestants 1500–1900.* Edinburgh, Clark.

HALL, MARIE BOAS (1991). *Promoting Experimental Learning: Experiment and the Royal Society 1660–1727.* Cambridge University Press.

HAMPTON, TIMOTHY (1990). *Writing from History: The Rhetoric of Exemplarity in Renaissance Literature.* Ithaca, NY, Cornell University Press.

HARDIE, COLIN (1976–77). 'Un cinquecento diece e cinque, *Purg.* 33, 43.' *Deutsches Dante Jahrbuch* (Cologne, Böhlau), 51–2: 84–98.

HARDIN, RICHARD F. (1992). *Civil Idolatry: Desacralizing and Monarchy in Spenser, Shakespeare, and Milton.* Cranbury, NJ: University of Delaware Press (c/o Associated University Presses).

HARDISON, O. B. (1977). 'Pythagoras and the Renaissance.' *Shakespeare Quarterly*, 28: 121–6.

HARINGTON, SIR JOHN (1930). *The Letters and Epigrams of Sir John Harington together with* The Praise of Private Life. Ed. Norman Egbert McClure. Philadelphia, University of Pennsylvania Press.

HARRISON, WILLIAM (1807). 'The Description of Britain.' In *Holinshed's Chronicles.* Ed. H. Ellis. i. London.

————— (1968). *The Description of England.* Ed. Georges Edelen. Ithaca, NY, Cornell University Press for the Folger Library.

HARVEY, GABRIEL (1913). *Gabriel Harvey's Marginalia.* Ed. G. C. Moore Smith. Stratford-upon-Avon, Shakespeare Head Press.

HASKELL, FRANCIS (1993). *History and its Images: Art and the Interpretation of the Past.* New Haven, Yale University Press.

HEARNE, THOMAS, ed. (1771). *A Collection of Curious Discourses, Written by Eminent Antiquaries upon Several Heads . . .* Ed. J. Ayloffe. 2 vols. London.

HEINE, HEINRICH (1827). *Buch der Lieder.* Hamburg.

HELD, JULIUS S. (1969). *Rembrandt's Aristotle and Other Rembrandt Studies*. Princeton University Press.

HENDERSON, JANICE ADRIENNE (1991). *On the Distances between Sun, Moon, and Earth According to Ptolemy, Copernicus and Reinhold*. Leiden, Brill.

HENINGER, S. K. (1968). 'Pythagorean Symbols in Erasmus' *Adagia*.' *Renaissance Quarterly*, 21: 162–5.

————— (1974). *Touches of Sweet Harmony: Pythagorean Cosmology and Renaissance Poetics*. San Marino, Calif., Huntington Library.

————— (1977). *The Cosmographical Glass: Renaissance Diagrams of the Universe*. San Marino, Calif., Huntington Library.

HENRY, JOHN, and HUTTON, SARAH, eds. (1990). *New Perspectives on Renaissance Thought: Essays in the History of Science, Education and Philosophy*. London, Duckworth.

HERBERT, GEORGE (1941). *The Works of George Herbert*. Ed. F. E. Hutchinson. Oxford, Clarendon Press.

HERFORD, C. H., and SIMPSON, PERCY and EVELYN (1925–52). *Ben Jonson*. 11 vols. Oxford, Clarendon Press.

Hermetica: The Ancient Greek and Latin Writings which Contain Religious or Philosophic Teachings Ascribed to Hermes Trismegistus (1985). Ed. and trans. Walter Scott. i. Boston, Mass., Shambhala.

Hermetica: The Greek Corpus Hermeticum and the Latin Asclepius in a New English Translation . . . (1992). Ed. Brian P. Copenhaver. Cambridge University Press.

HERRICK, ROBERT (1963). *Complete Poetry*. Ed. J. Max Patrick. New York University Press.

————— (1968). *The Poetical Works of Robert Herrick*. Ed. L. C. Martin. Rev. issue. Oxford, Clarendon Press.

HERSEY, GEORGE (1988). *The Lost Meaning of Classical Architecture: Speculations on Ornament from Vitruvius to Venturi*. Cambridge, Mass., MIT Press.

HEYWOOD, THOMAS (1990). *His Majesty's Royal Ship: A Critical Edition of Thomas Heywood's* A True Description *(1637)*. Ed. Alan R. Young. New York, AMS.

HIEATT, A. KENT (1983). 'The Genesis of Shakespeare's *Sonnets*: Spenser's *Ruines of Rome: by Bellay*.' *PMLA* 98: 800–14.

————— (1989). 'The Alleged Early Modern Origin of the Self and History: Terminate or Regroup?' *Spenser Studies*, 10: 1–36.

————— and PRESCOTT, ANNE LAKE (1992). 'Contemporizing

Antiquity: The *Hypnerotomachia* and its Afterlife in France.' *Word and Image*, 8: 291–321.

HIRSCH, JAMES E. (1981). *The Structure of Shakespearean Scenes*. New Haven, Yale University Press.

HODGE, R. I. (1978). *Foreshortened Time: Andrew Marvell and Seventeenth-Century Revolutions*. Cambridge, Brewer; Totowa, NJ: Rowman & Littlefield.

HOEFNAGEL, JORIS (1592). *Archetypa Studiaque*. With engravings by Jacob Hoefnagel. 4 vols. Frankfurt.

HOOYKAAS, R. (1976). 'The Reception of Copernicanism in England and the Netherlands.' In *The Anglo-Dutch Contribution to the Civilization of Early Modern Society*. London, Oxford University Press for the British Academy.

HOWARD, ALAN B. (1972). 'The World as Emblem: Language and Vision in the Poetry of Edward Taylor.' *American Literature*, 44: 359–84.

HOWARD, EDWARD (1705). *Copernicus Convicted*. London.

HOWARTH, DAVID (1985). *Lord Arundel and his Circle*. New Haven, Yale University Press.

————— (1992). 'Sir Robert Cotton and the Commemoration of Famous Men.' *British Library Journal*, 18: 1–28.

HOWARTH, HERBERT (1970). *The Tiger's Heart*. New York, Oxford University Press.

HOYNINGEN-HUENE, PAUL (1993). *Reconstructing Scientific Revolutions: Thomas S. Kuhn's Philosophy of Science*. Trans. Alexander T. Levine. Chicago University Press; Hemel Hempstead, IBD.

HUET, PIERRE DANIEL (1701). *Traitée de la situation du paradis terrestre, à Messieurs de l'Académie française*. Amsterdam.

HUGHES, MERRITT Y. (1965). *Ten Perspectives on Milton*. New Haven, Yale University Press.

HUGHES, ROBERT (1980). *The Shock of the New*. London, BBC.

HUIZINGA, JOHAN (1955). *The Waning of the Middle Ages* (1919). Trans. F. Hopman. Rev. edn. London, Penguin.

HULSE, CLARK (1988). 'Spenser, Bacon, and the Myth of Power.' In Heather Dubrow and Richard Strier, eds., *The Historical Renaissance: New Essays on Tudor and Stuart Literature and Culture*. University of Chicago Press.

HUNT, WILLIAM (1696). *Demonstration of Astrology; or, A Brief Discourse, Proving the Influence of the Sun, Moon, Stars, over this Terraqueous Globe:*

Grounded on the Fundamental Rules of the Copernican System . . . London.

HUTTAR, C. A. (1964). 'Old Testament Sainthood.' *Notes and Queries*, 209: 86–8.

HUTTON, RONALD (1991). *The Pagan Religions of the Ancient British Isles: Their Nature and Legacy.* Oxford, Blackwell.

HUYGENS, CHRISTIAAN (1698). *The Celestial Worlds Discovered* . . . London.

———— (1718). *Nouveau traité de la pluralité des mondes où l'on prouve par des raisons philosophiques que toutes les planètes sont habitées et cultivées comme notre terre.* Amsterdam.

Itinerarium Italicum (1975): *The Profile of the Italian Renaissance in the Mirror of its European Transformations: Dedicated to Paul Oskar Kristeller on the Occasion of his Seventieth Birthday.* Ed. Heiko A. Oberman. Leiden, Brill.

IVERSEN, ERIK (1968). *Obelisks in Exile*. i: *Obelisks of Rome.* Copenhagen, Gad.

JACK, RONALD D. S. (1989). *Patterns of Divine Comedy: A Study of Medieval English Drama.* Cambridge, Brewer.

JAYNE, SEARS (1983). *Library Catalogues of the English Renaissance.* Rev. edn. Godalming, St Paul's Bibliographies.

JOHNSON, FRANCIS RARICK (1937). *Astronomical Thought in Renaissance England.* Baltimore, Johns Hopkins University Press.

JONES, KAREN SPARCK (1986). *Synonymy and Semantic Classification.* Edinburgh Information Technology Series, 1. Edinburgh University Press.

JONES, RICHARD FOSTER (1961). *Ancients and Moderns: A Study of the Rise of the Scientific Movement in Seventeenth-Century England.* Rev. edn. St Louis, Mo., Washington University Press.

JONSON, BEN (1975). *Poems.* Ed. Ian Donaldson. London, Oxford University Press.

JOURDAIN, M. (1904). *Translations of the Odes of Horace Collected and Arranged.* London, Dent.

JUNG, C. G. (1953). *Psychology and Alchemy.* Trans. R. F. C. Hull. London, Routledge & Kegan Paul.

———— (1963). *Memories, Dreams, and Reflections.* Ed. Aniela Jaffé. Trans. Richard and Clara Winston. London, Routledge.

———— (1968). *The Archetypes and the Collective Unconscious.* Trans. R. F. C. Hull. Rev. edn. London, Routledge & Kegan Paul.

KAHN, VICTORIA ANN (1985). *Rhetoric, Prudence, and Scepticism in the Renaissance*. Ithaca, NY, Cornell University Press.

KEEN, MAURICE (1977). 'Huizinga, Kilgour and the Decline of Chivalry.' *Medievalia et Humanistica*, NS 8: *Tranformation and Continuity*, ed. Paul Maurice Clogan. Cambridge University Press.

—————— (1984). *Chivalry.* New Haven, Yale University Press.

KEMP, ANTHONY (1991). *The Estrangement of the Past: A Study in the Origins of Modern Historical Consciousness*. New York, Oxford University Press.

KEMP, MARTIN (1992). *The Science of Art*. New Haven, Yale University Press.

KEPLER, JOHANNES (1634). *Somnium, seu Opus Posthumum de Astronomia Lunari . . .* Frankfurt.

KERRIGAN, JOHN (1988). 'Thomas Carew.' Chatterton Lecture. *Proceedings of the British Academy*, 74: 311–50.

KERRIGAN, WILLIAM, and BRADEN, GORDON (1989). *The Idea of the Renaissance*. Baltimore, Johns Hopkins University Press.

KILGOUR, R. L. (1937). *The Decline of Chivalry.* Cambridge, Mass., Harvard University Press.

KING, HENRY (1965). *Poems*. Ed. Margaret Crum. Oxford, Clarendon Press.

KING, JOHN N. (1989). *Tudor Royal Iconography: Literature and Art in an Age of Religious Crisis*. Princeton University Press.

KIPLING, GORDON (1977). *The Triumph of Honour: Burgundian Origins of the Elizabethan Renaissance*. Leiden, Sir Thomas Browne Institute.

KIRCHER, FR. ATHANASIUS (1656). *Itinerarium Exstaticum*. Rome.

——————. *See* Merrill, Brian L.

KOCHER, P. H. (1953). *Science and Religion in Elizabethan England*. San Marino, Calif.: Huntington Library.

KOENIGSBERGER, DOROTHY (1971). *Renaissance Man and Creative Thinking: A History of Concepts of Harmony 1400–1700*. Hassocks, Harvester Press.

KOSELLECK, REINHART (1985). *Futures Past: On the Semantics of Historical Time*. Trans. Keith Tribe. Cambridge, Mass., MIT Press.

KOSTOFF, SPIRO (1991). *The City Shaped: Urban Patterns and Meanings through History.* London, Thames & Hudson.

KOYRÉ, ALEXANDRE (1958). *From the Closed World to the Infinite Universe*. Repr. New York, Harper.

KREMEN, KATHRYN R. (1972). *The Imagination of the Resurrection.* Lewisburg, Penn., Bucknell University Press.

KROLL, RICHARD, ASHCRAFT, RICHARD and ZAGORIN, PEREZ, eds. (1992). *Philosophy, Science and Religion in England 1640–1700.* Cambridge University Press.

KUBOVY, MICHAEL (1986). *The Psychology of Perspective and Renaissance Art.* Cambridge University Press.

KUHN, THOMAS S. (1977). 'Mathematical versus Experimental Traditions in the Development of Physical Science.' In *The Essential Tension: Selected Studies in Scientific Tradition and Change.* University of Chicago Press.

——— (1985). *The Copernican Revolution* (1957). Rev. edn. Cambridge, Mass., Harvard University Press.

KUILE, ONNO TER (1985). *Seventeenth-Century North Netherlandish Still Lifes.* The Hague, Staatsuitgeverij; Amsterdam, Meulenhoff/ Landshoff.

KUIN, ROGER (1989). 'Sir Philip Sidney: The Courtier and the Text.' *English Literary Renaissance*, 19: 249–71.

L'ORANGE, HANS PETER (1953). *Studies on the Iconography of Cosmic Kingship in the Ancient World.* Oslo, Aschehoug.

——— (1982). *Apotheosis in Ancient Portraiture* (1947). Repr. New Rochelle, NY, Caratzas.

LADIS, ANDREW (1982). *Taddeo Gaddi.* Columbia, Missouri University Press.

LAKOFF, GEORGE, and JOHNSON, MARK (1980). *Metaphors we Live By.* Chicago University Press.

LANDAU, SIDNEY I. (1989). *Dictionaries: The Art and Craft of Lexicography.* Repr. Cambridge University Press.

LAZZARO, CLAUDIA (1990). *The Italian Renaissance Garden: From the Conventions of Planting, Design and Ornament to the Grand Gardens of Sixteenth-Century Central Italy.* New Haven, Yale University Press.

LE GOFF, JACQUES (1988a). *Medieval Civilization 400–1500.* Trans. Julia Barrow. Oxford, Blackwell.

——— (1988b). *The Medieval Imagination.* Trans. Arthur Goldhammer. Chicago University Press.

LEHMANN, KARL (1945). 'The Dome of Heaven.' *Art Bulletin*, 27: 1–27.

LEIGH, RICHARD (1947). *Poems by Richard Leigh (1675).* Ed. Hugh Macdonald. Oxford, Blackwell.

LEONARD, JOHN (1990). *Naming in Paradise: Milton and the Language of Adam and Eve.* Oxford, Clarendon Press.

LESLIE, MICHAEL (1983). *Spenser's 'Fierce Warres and Faithfull Loves': Martial and Chivalric Symbolism in The Faerie Queene.* Cambridge, Brewer; Totowa, NJ, Barnes & Noble.

LESSING, DORIS (1981). *The Marriages between Zones Three, Four, and Five.* London, Granada.

LEVY, F. J. (1967). *Tudor Historical Thought.* San Marino, Calif., Huntington Library.

LEWALSKI, BARBARA KIEFER (1973). *Donne's* Anniversaries *and the Poetry of Praise: The Creation of a Symbolic Mode.* Princeton University Press.

LIVINGSTON, PAISLEY (1991). *Literary Knowledge: Humanistic Inquiry and the Philosophy of Science.* Ithaca, NY, Cornell University Press.

LLEWELLYN, NIGEL (1990). 'Claims to Status through Visual Codes: Heraldry on Post-Reformation Funeral Monuments.' In Anglo (1990: 145–60).

———— (1991). *The Art of Death: Visual Culture in the English Death Ritual c.1500–c.1800.* London, Reaktion and Victoria and Albert Museum.

LOHR, CHARLES H. (1974). 'Renaissance Latin Aristotle Commentaries: Authors A–B'. *Studies in the Renaissance,* 21: 228–89.

———— (1975). 'Renaissance Latin Aristotle Commentaries: Authors C.' *Renaissance Quarterly,* 28: 674–89.

LORGUES–LAPOUGE, CHRISTIANE (1957). 'Triomphes Renaissants.' *L'Œil,* 35: 26–35.

LOVEJOY, ARTHUR O. (1936). *The Great Chain of Being: A Study of the History of an Idea.* Cambridge, Mass., Harvard University Press.

LYONS, JOHN D., and NICHOLS, STEPHEN G., Jr., eds. (1982). *Mimesis, from Mirror to Method: Augustine to Descartes.* Hanover, NH: University Press of New England.

LYTE, HENRY (1588). *The Light of Britain: A Record of the Honourable Original and Antiquity of Britain.* London.

MCCANLES, MICHAEL (1992). *Jonsonian Discriminations: The Humanist Poet and the Praise of True Nobility.* University of Toronto Press.

MCDANNELL, COLLEEN, and LANG, BERNHARD (1988). *Heaven: A History.* New Haven, Yale University Press.

MACDONALD, ROBERT R., ed. (1984). *The Sun King: Louis XIV and the*

New World. Exhibition Catalogue. New Orleans, Louisiana Museum Foundation.

MACDOUGAL, HUGH A. (1982). *Racial Myth in English History: Trojans, Teutons, and Anglo-Saxons*. Montreal, Harvest House; Hanover, NH, University Press of New England.

MACE, DEAN TOLLE (1985). 'Transformations in Classical Art Theory: From "Poetic Composition" to "Picturesque Composition".' *Word and Image* 1: 59–86.

MCFARLANE, IAN D. (1986). 'The Renaissance Epitaph.' *Modern Language Review.* 81: 1–11.

MACK, MAYNARD (1985). *Alexander Pope: A Life*. New Haven, Yale University Press; New York, Norton.

MCKNIGHT, STEPHEN A. (1991). *The Modern Age and the Recovery of Ancient Wisdom: A Reconsideration of Historical Consciousness 1450–1650*. Columbia, University of Missouri Press.

MCMANNERS, JOHN (1981). *Death and the Enlightenment: Changing Attitudes to Death among Christians and Unbelievers in Eighteenth-Century France*. Oxford, Clarendon Press.

MACQUEEN, JOHN (1985). *Numerology: Theory and Outline History of a Literary Mode*. Edinburgh University Press.

MACROBIUS (1952). *Commentary on the Dream of Scipio*. Ed. William Harris Stahl. New York, Columbia University Press.

MAIORINO, GIANCARLO (1987). *Adam 'New Born and Perfect': The Renaissance Promise of Eternity*. Bloomington, Indiana University Press.

———— (1990). *The Cornucopian Mind and the Baroque Unity of the Arts*. University Park, Pennsylvania State University Press.

MANDROU, ROBERT (1978). *From Humanism to Science 1480–1700*. Trans. Brian Pearce. London, Penguin.

MANGANELLI, GIORGIO (1989). 'Let Us Build Us a Tower: The Desert of Namelessness.' Trans. Jonathan Keates. With notes on paintings reproduced, by Alessandro Tosi, trans. Jeanne Chapman. *FMR* No. 36: 1–24.

MANLEY, FRANK (1963). *John Donne: The Anniversaries*. Baltimore, Johns Hopkins University Press.

MANNING, R. JOHN (1985). 'Rule and Order Strange: A Reading of Sir John Davies' *Orchestra*.' *English Literary Renaissance*, 15: 175–94.

MANUEL, FRANK E. (1963). *Isaac Newton, Historian*. Cambridge, Mass., Harvard University Press/Belknap.

———— and MANUEL, FRITZIE P. (1979). *Utopian Thought in the*

Western World. Cambridge, Mass., Harvard University Press/ Belknap.

MARLE, RAIMOND VAN (1931–2). *Iconographie de l'art profane.* 2 vols. The Hague, Nijhoff.

MARROW, JAMES H., DEFOER, HENRI L. M., KORTEWEG, ANNE S., and WÜSTEFELD, WILHELMINA C. M. (1990). *The Golden Age of Dutch Manuscript Painting.* New York, Braziller.

MARTIN, JULIAN (1992). *Francis Bacon, the State, and the Reform of Natural Philosophy.* Cambridge University Press.

MARTINDALE, CHARLES (1988). *Ovid Renewed: Ovidian Influences on Literature and Art from the Middle Ages to the Twentieth Century.* Cambridge University Press.

MARVELL, ANDREW (1971). *The Poems and Letters of Andrew Marvell.* Ed. H. M. Margoliouth. Rev. Pierre Legouis and E. Duncan-Jones. 2 vols. Oxford, Clarendon Press.

MASSIN (1970). *Letter and Image.* Trans. Caroline Hillier and Vivienne Menkes. London, Studio Vista.

MEBANE, JOHN S. (1989). *Renaissance Magic and the Return of the Golden Age: The Occult Tradition and Marlowe, Jonson, and Shakespeare.* Lincoln, University of Nebraska Press.

MEISS, MILLARD (1969). *French Painting in the Time of Jean de Berry.* 2 vols. Rev. edn. London, Phaidon.

MELTON, EDWARD (1681). *Zeldzame en Gedenkwaardige Zee en Land Reizen.* Amsterdam.

MERRILL, BRIAN L., ed. (1989). *Athanasius Kircher (1602–1680) . . . An Exhibition of his Works.* Provo, Utah, Brigham Young University Library.

MERTES, KATE (1988). *The English Noble Household 1250–1600: Good Governance and Politic Rule.* Oxford, Blackwell.

MERTON, R. I. (1938). *Science, Technology and Society in Seventeenth Century England.* Bruges, St Catherine Press.

MESEROLE, HARRISON T., ed. (1968). *Seventeenth-Century American Poetry.* New York, Norton.

MIDDLETON, ARTHUR (1992). *Globes of the Western World.* London, Sotheby's.

MIDDLETON, CHRISTOPHER (1976). *The History of Heaven: Poetical Fictions of All the Stars* (1596). Facs. Amsterdam, Theatrum Orbis Terrarum.

MILLER, JAMES (1985). *Measures of Wisdom.* Toronto University Press.

MILTON, JOHN (1971). *Paradise Lost*. Ed. Alastair Fowler. London, Longman.

MINKOWSKI, HELMUT (1991). *Vermutungen: uber den Turm zu Babel*. Freren, Luca.

MINNIS, ALASTAIR J. (1977). 'Discussions of "Authorial Role" and "Literary Form" in Late-Medieval Scriptural Exegesis.' In *Beiträge zur Geschichte der Deutschen Sprache und Literatur*. Tübingen, Niemeyer.

———— (1982). *Chaucer and Pagan Antiquity*. Chaucer Studies, 8. Cambridge, Brewer.

———— (1984). *Medieval Theory of Authorship*. London, Scolar Press.

MIRANDOLA, PICO DELLA (1965). *On the Dignity of Man, On Being and the One, Heptaplus*. Trans. Charles Glenn Wallis, Paul J. W. Miller, and Douglas Carmichael. Ed. Paul J. W. Miller. Repr. Indianapolis, Bobbs-Merrill.

———— *Disputationes adversus Astrologiam Divinatricem*. Ed. E. Garin. 2 vols. Florence, 1973.

MITFORD, NANCY (1966). *The Sun King: Louis XIV at Versailles*. New York, Harper.

MONTAIGNE, MICHEL DE (1910). *The Essayes . . .* Trans. John Florio. 3 vols. London, Dent.

———— (1958). *The Complete Works of Montaigne: Essays, Travel Journal, Letters*. Trans. and ed. Donald M. Frame. London, Hamilton.

———— (1993). *The Complete Essays*. Trans. and ed. M. A. Screech. London, Penguin.

MORE, HENRY (1966). *Opera Omnia* (1674–9). Ed. Serge Hutin. 3 vols. Repr. Hildesheim, Olms.

———— (1987). *The Immortality of the Soul*. Ed. A. Jacob. Dordrecht, Nijhoff.

MORFORD, MARK (1987). 'The Stoic Garden.' *Journal of Garden History*, 7: 151–75.

MORGAN, VICTOR (1983). 'The Literary Image of Globes and Maps in Early Modern England.' In Sarah Tyacke, ed., *English Map-Making 1500–1650: Historical Essays*. London, British Library.

MOSELEY, CHARLES (1989). *A Century of Emblems: An Introductory Anthology*. Aldershot, Scolar Press.

MOSS, JEAN DIETZ (1993). *Novelties in the Heavens: Rhetoric and Science in the Copernican Controversy*. Chicago University Press; Hemel Hempstead, IBD.

MUIR, KENNETH (1979). *Shakespeare's Sonnets*. London, Allen & Unwin.

MUNDY, PETER (1907–36). *The Travels of Peter Mundy in Europe and Asia 1608–1667*. Ed. Sir Richard Carnac Temple. 6 vols. Cambridge University Press for the Hakluyt Society.

MURPHY, AVON JACK (1972). 'The Critical Elegy of Earlier Seventeenth-Century England.' *Genre*, 5: 75–105.

NEWBERY, TIMOTHY J., BISACCA, GEORGE, and KANTER, LAWRENCE B. (1990). *Italian Renaissance Frames*. New York, Abrams for the Metropolitan Museum of art.

NEYMAN, JERZY, ed. (1977). *The Heritage of Copernicus: Theories 'Pleasing to the Mind'*. Cambridge, Mass., MIT Press.

NICHOLS, FRANCIS MORGAN, ed. (1986). *The Marvels of Rome: 'Mirabilia Urbis Romae'*. New York, Italica.

NICOLESCU, BASARAB (1991). Trans. R. Baker. *Science, Meaning, and Evolution: The Cosmology of Jacob Boehme*. Repr. New York, Parabola Books.

NICOLSON, MARJORIE HOPE (1961). *Voyages to the Moon*. West Drayton, Collier-Macmillan.

———— (1985). *The Breaking of the Circle: Studies in the Effect of the 'New Science' upon Seventeenth-Century Poetry* (1950). Repr. New York, Octagon.

NORBROOK, DAVID (1984). *Poetry and Politics in the English Renaissance*. London, Routledge.

NORTH, JOHN (1988). *Chaucer's Universe*. Oxford, Clarendon Press.

———— (1989). *The Universal Frame: Historical Essays in Astronomy Natural Philosophy and Scientific Method*. London, Hambledon.

NUTTALL, ANTHONY DAVID. (1983). *A New Mimesis: Shakespeare and the Representation of Reality*. London, Methuen.

OLDHAM, JOHN (1987). *The Poems*. Ed. Harold F. Brooks with Raman Selden. Oxford, Clarendon Press.

ONIANS, JOHN (1988). *Bearers of Meaning: The Classical Orders in Antiquity, the Middle Ages, and the Renaissance*. Princeton University Press.

ORBISON, T. (1983). 'The Middle Temple Documents Relating to James Shirley's *Triumph of Peace*.' *Malone Society Collections*, 12: 31–84.

ORGEL, STEPHEN, and STRONG, SIR ROY (1973). *Inigo Jones: The*

Theatre of the Stuart Court . . . London, Sotheby Parke Bernet; Berkeley, University of California Press.

ORRELL, JOHN (1985). *The Theatres of Inigo Jones and John Webb.* Cambridge University Press.

OVID (1961). *The XV Books of P. Ovidius Naso, Entitled Metamorphosis.* Trans. Arthur Golding (1567). Ed. W. H. D. Rouse. London, Centaur. *For Ovid, see also* Anon. (1920), Bersuire (1511).

PAGE, R. I. (1977). 'Christopher Marlowe and the Library of Matthew Parker.' *Notes and Queries*, 122: 510–14.

PALINGENIO, MARCELLO (1574). *Zodiacus Vitae.* London.

———— (1947). *The Zodiac of Life.* Trans. Barnaby Googe (1560). New York, Scholars' Facsimiles and Reprints.

PALISCA, C. V. (1956). 'Vincenzo Galilei's Counterpoint Treatise: A Code for the *Seconda Practica.*' *Journal of the American Musicological Society*, 9: 81–96.

PANOFSKY, ERWIN (1955). *Meaning in the Visual Arts: Papers in and on Art History.* Garden City, NY, Doubleday.

———— (1970). *Renaissance and Renascences in Western Art.* Rev. edn. London, Granada.

PARRY, G. J. R. (1987). *A Protestant Vision, William Harrison and the Reformation of Elizabethan England.* Cambridge University Press.

PARRY, GRAHAM (1980). *Hollar's England: A Mid-Seventeenth-Century View.* London, Russell.

———— (1981). *The Golden Age Restored: The Culture of the Stuart Court 1603–1642.* Manchester University Press.

PATRIDES, C. A. (1966). *Milton and the Christian Tradition.* Oxford, Clarendon Press.

———— (1982). *Premises and Motifs in Renaissance Thought and Literature.* Princeton University Press.

———— and WITTREICH, JOSEPH (1984). *The Apocalypse in English Renaissance Thought and Literature.* Manchester University Press.

PATTERSON, RICHARD (1981). 'The "Hortus Palatinus" at Heidelberg and the Reformation of the World.' *Journal of Garden History*, 1: 67–104, 179–202.

PAULY, AUGUST FRIEDRICH VON, and WISSOWA, GEORG (1893–). *Paulys Realencyclopädie der classischen Altertumswissenschaft.* 34 vols. with suppl. Stuttgart, Metzlerscher Verlag; Druckenmüller.

PAXTON, FREDERICK S. (1990). *Christianizing Death: The Creation of a*

Ritual Process in Early Medieval Europe. Ithaca, NY, Cornell University Press.

PEACHAM, HENRY (1906). *Peacham's Complete Gentleman* (London, 1622). Ed. G. S. Gordon. Facs of 1634 edn. Oxford, Clarendon Press.

PEACOCK, JOHN (1987). 'Jonson and Jones Collaborate on *Prince Henry's Barriers.*' *Word and Image*, 3: 172–94.

PELIKAN, JAROSLAV JAN (1961). *The Shape of Death: Life, Death and Immortality in the Early Fathers.* New York, Abingdon Press.

PETRARCA, FRANCESCO (1966). 'On the Fame of Writers.' In *Four Dialogues for Scholars.* Trans. and ed. Conrad H. Rawski. Cleveland, Western Reserve University Press.

PHILIP, J. A. (1966). *Pythagoras and Early Pythagoreanism. Phoenix: Journal of the Classical Association of Canada,* suppl. vol. 7. University of Toronto.

PHILIPOTT, THOMAS (1950). *Poems (1646).* Liverpool University Press.

PICCOLOMINI, ALISANDRO (1548). *De la Sfera del Mondo . . . De le Stelle Fisse.* Venice.

PIGGOTT, STUART (1976). *Ruins in a Landscape: Essays in Antiquarianism.* Edinburgh University Press.

PINGREE, DAVID (1986). *Picatrix: The Latin Version of the* Ghayat Al-Hakim. Studies of the Warburg Institute, 39. London, Warburg and Courtauld Institute.

PLUMB, JOHN HAROLD (1969). *The Death of the Past.* London, Macmillan; Boston, Houghton Mifflin.

POMPONAZZI, PIETRO (1948). *On Immortality.* Trans. William Henry Hay II and John Herman Randall, Jr. Ed. Paul Oskar Kristeller. In Ernst Cassirer, Paul Oskar Kristeller, and John Herman Randall, Jr., eds., *The Renaissance Philosophy of Man.* University of Chicago Press.

POPKIN, RICHARD H. (1991). *The Third Force in Seventeenth Century Thought.* Leiden, Brill.

PORPHYRY (1991). *On the Cave of the Nymphs.* Trans. Thomas Taylor. Grand Rapids, Mich., Phanes.

PRAZ, MARIO (1964). *Studies in Seventeenth-Century Imagery.* Rev. edn. Rome, Edizioni di Storia e Letteratura.

PREST, JOHN (1981). *The Garden of Eden: The Botanic Garden and the Re-creation of Paradise.* New Haven, Yale University Press.

PUMFREY, STEPHEN, ROSSI, PAOLO, and SLAWINSKI, MAURICE,

eds. (1991). *Science, Culture and Popular Belief in Renaissance Europe.* Manchester University Press.

QUARLES, FRANCIS (1960). *Hosanna; or, Divine Poems on the Passion of Christ; Threnodes.* Ed. John Horden. Liverpool University Press.

QUINONES, RICARDO J. (1972). *The Renaissance Discovery of Time.* Cambridge, Mass., Harvard University Press.

RABINOWITZ, PETER J. (1987). *Before Reading: Narrative Conventions and the Politics of Interpretation.* Ithaca, NY, Cornell University Press.

RAIMARUS, NICOLAUS (Reymers) (1588). *Fundamentum Astronomicum.* Strasbourg.

RANALD, MARGARET LOFTUS (1987). *Shakespeare and his Social Context: Essays in Osmotic Knowledge and Literary Interpretation.* New York, AMS Press.

RANDALL, LILIAN M. C. (1974). 'Pea-Pods and Molluscs from the Master of Catherine of Cleves Workshop.' *Apollo,* 100/153: 26–33.

RATHBORNE, ISABEL E. (1937). *The Meaning of Spenser's Fairyland.* New York, Columbia University Press.

REDONDI, P. (1987). *Galileo, Heretic.* Trans. R. Rosenthal. Princeton University Press.

REEVES, MARJORIE, ed. (1992). *Prophetic Rome in the High Renaissance Period.* Oxford, Clarendon Press.

REISS, TIMOTHY J. (1992). Review of Timothy Hampton, *Writing from History. Modern Philology,* 90: 255–8.

RHYS, HEDLEY HOWELL, ed. (1961). *Seventeenth Century Science and the Arts.* Princeton University Press.

RICCIOLI, GIOVANNI-BATTISTA (1651). *Novum Almagestum.* Rome.

RICŒUR, PAUL (1984). *Time and Narrative.* Trans. Kathleen McLaughlin and David Pellauer. Chicago University Press.

RIFKIN, JEREMY (1987). *Time Wars: The Primary Conflict in Human History.* New York, Holt.

RIPA, CESARE (1976). *Iconologia (Padua 1611).* Facs. New York, Garland.

RIVERS, ISABEL (1991). *Reason, Grace and Sentiment: A Study of the Language of Religion and Ethics in England 1660–1780.* i: *Whichcote to Wesley.* Cambridge University Press.

ROBERTS, JULIAN, and WATSON, ANDREW G. (1990). *John Dee's Library Catalogue.* Oxford University Press for London Bibliography Society.

156 REFERENCES

ROCHE, THOMAS P., Jr. (1989). *Petrarch and the English Sonnet Sequences.* New York, AMS.

ROGERS, PAT, ed. (1987). *Oxford Illustrated History of English Literature.* Oxford, Oxford University Press.

ROGERS, PHILIP GEORGE (1966). *The Fifth Monarchy Men.* London, Oxford University Press.

RORTY, RICHARD (1980). *Philosophy and the Mirror of Nature.* Rev. edn. Princeton University Press.

RÖSLIN, HELISAEUS (1597). *De Opere Dei Creationis . . .* Frankfurt.

RØSTVIG, MAREN-SOFIE (1954). *The Happy Man: Studies in the Metamorphoses of a Classical Ideal 1600–1700.* Oslo, Akademisk Forlag; Oxford, Blackwell.

———— (1971). *The Happy Man: Studies in the Metamorphoses of a Classical Ideal.* i: *1600–1700.* Rev. edn. Oslo, Norwegian Universities Press.

———— (1994). *Configurations: A Topomorphical Approach to Renaissance Poetry.* Oslo, Scandinavian University Press.

ROWAN, ANN MARTHA (1974). *Laurieston Castle.* Oldhill, Dunstable, ABC Historic Publications.

RUMRICH, JOHN PETER (1987). *Matter of Glory: A New Preface to Paradise Lost.* Pittsburgh, Penn., University of Pittsburgh Press.

RUSSELL, DANIEL S. (1985). *The Emblem and Device in France.* Lexington, Ky., French Forum.

SAINTSBURY, GEORGE (1905). *Minor Poets of the Caroline Period.* 3 vols. Oxford, Clarendon Press.

SALMON, VIVIEN (1972). *The Works of Francis Lodwick: A Study of his Writings in the Intellectual Context of the Seventeenth Century.* London, Longman.

SAXL, FRITZ (1939). 'Pagan Sacrifice in the Italian Renaissance.' *Journal of the Warburg Institute,* 2: 346–67.

SCHAMA, SIMON (1987). *The Embarrassment of Riches: An Interpretation of Dutch Culture in the Golden Age.* London, Collins.

SCHEINER, CHRISTOPHER ('Appelles') (1613). *De Maculis Solaribus.* Rome.

SCHERER, MARGARET R. (1955). *Marvels of Ancient Rome.* New York, Phaidon for the Metropolitan Museum of Art.

SCHICKARD, WILHELM (1655). *Atlas.* Nördlingen.

SCHILLER, JULIUS (1660). *Atlas Caelestis seu Harmonia Macrocosmica.* Amsterdam.

SCHNEIDER, NORBERT (1990). *The Art of the Still Life: Still Life Painting in the Early Modern Period.* Trans. Hugh Beyer. Cologne, Taschen.

SCHOLZ, B. F. (1988). 'Jacob Cats' *Silenus Alcibiadis* in 1618 and in 1862: Changes in Word–Image Relations from the Seventeenth to the Nineteenth Century.' *Word and Image,* 4: 67–80.

SCHULER, ROBERT M. (1985). 'Theory and Criticism of the Scientific Poem in Elizabethan England.' *English Literary Renaissance,* 15: 3–41.

SCHULTZ, HOWARD (1955). *Milton and Forbidden Knowledge.* New York, Modern Language Association.

SCOTT, ALAN B. (1991). *Origen and the Life of the Stars: A History of an Idea.* Oxford, Clarendon.

SEGRE, MICHAEL (1991). *In the Wake of Galileo.* New Brunswick, NJ, Rutgers University Press.

SENN, WERNER (1989). 'Speaking the Silence: Contemporary Poems on Paintings.' *Word and Image,* 5: 181–97.

SERLIO, SEBASTIANO (1964). *Tutte l'Opere d'Architettura, et Prospetiva* . . . (Venice, 1619). Repr. Ridgewood, NJ, Gregg.

SESTI, GIUSEPPE MARIA (1991). *The Glorious Constellations: History and Mythology.* New York, Abrams.

SEZNEC, JEAN (1953). *The Survival of the Pagan Gods: The Mythological Tradition and its Place in Renaissance Humanism and Art.* Trans. Barbara F. Sessions. New York, Pantheon for the Bollingen Foundation.

SHAPIRO, BARBARA (1983). *Probability and Certainty in Seventeenth-Century England: A Study of the Relationships between Natural Science, Religion, History, Law, and Literature.* Princeton University Press.

SHARPE, KEVIN (1987). *Criticism and Compliment: The Politics of Literature in the England of Charles I.* Cambridge University Press.

SHEA, WILLIAM R. (1972). *Galileo's Intellectual Revolution.* London, Macmillan.

SHRIMPLIN-EVANGELIDIS, VALERIE (1990). 'Sun-Symbolism and Cosmology in Michelangelo's *Last Judgement*'. *Sixteenth-Century Journal,* 21: 607–44.

SHUMAKER, WAYNE (1972). *The Occult Sciences: A Study in Intellectual Patterns.* Berkeley, University of California Press.

SIDNEY, SIR PHILIP (1987). *The Countess of Pembroke's Arcadia (The New Arcadia).* Ed. Victor Skretkowicz. Oxford, Clarendon Press.

SKRETKOWICZ, VICTOR (1982). 'Symbolic Architecture in Sidney's *New Arcadia*'. *Review of English Studies,* NS 33: 175–80.

SLOANE, THOMAS O. (1985). *Donne, Milton, and the End of Humanist Rhetoric*. Berkeley, University of California Press.

SMARR, JANET LEVARIE (1984). 'The Pyramid and the Circle: "Ovid's Banquet of Sense".' *Philological Quarterly*, 63: 369–86.

SMITH, A. J. (1985). 'Sacred Earth: Metaphysical Poetry and the Advance of Science.' *Proceedings of the British Academy*, 71: 251–66.

SMITH, E. BALDWIN (1971). *The Dome: A Study in the History of Ideas* (1950). Repr. Princeton University Press.

SMITH, NIGEL (1989). *Perfection Proclaimed: Language and Literature in English Radical Religion 1640–1660*. Oxford, Clarendon Press; New York, Oxford University Press.

SMITH, WILLIAM (1688). *A Future World in which Mankind shall Survive their Mortal Durations Demonstrated by Rational Evidence from Natural and Moral Arguments against the Atheists' Pretensions . . .* London.

SNYDER, SUSAN (1979). *The Comic Matrix of Shakespeare's Tragedies*. Princeton University Press.

SNYDER, GEORGE SERGEANT (1984). *Maps of the Heavens*. London, Deutsch.

SOMERSET, FITZROY RICHARD, BARON RAGLAN (1964). *The Temple and the House*. London, Routledge & Kegan Paul.

SOUTHERN, R. W. (1994). *Scholastic Humanism and the Unification of Europe*. i: *Foundations*. Oxford, Blackwell.

SOUTHGATE, B. C. (1990). ' "No Other Wisdom"? Humanist Reactions to Science and Scientism in the Seventeenth Century.' *The Seventeenth Century*, 5: 71–92.

SPENSER, EDMUND (1977). *The Faerie Queene*. Ed. A. C. Hamilton. London, Longman.

SPERBER, DAN, and WILSON, DEIRDRE (1986). *Relevance*. Cambridge, Mass., Harvard University Press.

STANLEY, THOMAS (1660). *The History of Philosophy: The Third and Last Volume, in Five Parts*. London.

STERNFELD, FREDERICK W., and GREER, DAVID, eds. (1967). *E. H. Fellowes: English Madrigal Verse 1588–1632*. 3rd edn. Oxford, Clarendon Press.

STEPHENSON, BRUCE (1994). *The Music of the Heavens: Kepler's Harmonic Astronomy*. Princeton University Press.

STEVENS, PAUL (1989). 'Subversion and Wonder in Milton's Epitaph "On Shakespeare".' *English Literary Renaissance*, 19: 375–88.

STRONG, SIR ROY (1979). *The Renaissance Garden in England*. London, Thames & Hudson.

———— (1986). *Henry, Prince of Wales and England's Lost Renaissance.* London, Thames & Hudson.

———— (1987). *Gloriana: The Portraits of Queen Elizabeth I.* London, Thames & Hudson.

———— *See also* Orgel and Strong (1973).

SUCKLING, SIR JOHN (1971). *The Works.* i: *The Non-Dramatic Works.* Ed. T. Clayton. Oxford, Clarendon Press.

SUMMERSON, SIR JOHN (1963). *Heavenly Mansions and Other Essays on Architecture.* New York, Norton.

SUTHERLAND, SARAH P. (1983). *Masques in Jacobean Tragedy.* New York, AMS.

SUTTON, PETER C. (1992). *Dutch and Flemish Seventeenth-Century Paintings: The Harold Samuel Collection.* Cambridge University Press.

———— *et al.* (1987). *Masters of Seventeenth-Century Dutch Landscape Painting.* London, Herbert.

SWARDSON, H. R. (1962). *Poetry and the Fountain of Light: Observations on the Conflict between Christian and Classical Traditions in Seventeenth-Century Poetry.* London, Allen & Unwin.

SYLVESTER, JOSHUA (1880). *The Complete Works of Joshua Sylvester.* Ed. Alexander B. Grosart. 2 vols. Chertsey Worthies' Library. Edinburgh, privately printed.

SYME, SIR RONALD (1960). *The Roman Revolution.* Oxford University Press.

TATON, RENÉ, and WILSON, CURTIS, eds. (1989). *The General History of Astronomy.* ii: *Planetary Astronomy from the Renaissance to the Rise of Astrophysics.* Pt. A: *Tycho Brahe to Newton.* Cambridge University Press.

TAUB, LIBA CHAIA (1993). *Ptolemy's Universe: The Natural Philosophical and Ethical Foundations of Ptolemy's Astronomy.* La Salle, Ill., Open Court.

TEMPORINI, HILDEGARD, and HAASE, W. (1972–). *Aufstieg und Niedergang der Römischen Welt. Geschichte und Kultur Roms im Spiegel der neueren Forschung.* Berlin and New York, De Gruyter.

TERVARENT, GUY DE (1958). *Attributs et symboles dans l'art profane 1450–1600: Dictionnaire d'un langage perdu.* Travaux d'Humanisme et Renaissance, 29. Geneva, Droz.

THOMAS, SIR KEITH (1988). *Religion and the Decline of Magic: Studies in Popular Beliefs in Sixteenth- and Seventeenth-Century England* (1971). Repr. London, Penguin.

THOMPSON, CHARLOTTE (1985). 'Love in an Orderly Universe: A Unification of Spenser's *Amoretti*, "Anacreontics", and *Epithalamion*.' *Viator*, 16: 277–335.

THOREN, VICTOR E. (1990). *The Lord of Uraniborg: A Biography of Tycho Brahe*. Cambridge University Press.

THORN-DRURY, GEORGE (1921). *A Little Ark Containing Sundry Pieces of Seventeenth-Century Verse*. London, Dobell.

THRUPP, SYLVIA LETTICE, ed. (1964). *Change in Medieval Society: Europe North of the Alps 1050–1500*. New York, Appleton-Century-Crofts.

TILLOTSON, JOHN (1696–1735). *The Works . . .* 3 vols. London.

TILLYARD, E. M. W. (1960). *English Renaissance*. London, Hogarth.

TREVOR-ROPER, HUGH R. (Baron Dacre of Glanton) (1969). *The European Witch-Craze of the Sixteenth and Seventeenth Centuries and Other Essays*. Repr. New York, Harper & Row.

———— (1985). *Renaissance Essays*. Chicago University Press.

———— (1987). *Catholics, Anglicans and Puritans: Seventeenth Century Essays*. London, Secker & Warburg.

TRINKAUS, CHARLES EDWARD (1983). *The Scope of Renaissance Humanism*. Ann Arbor, University of Michigan Press.

TUFTE, EDWARD R. (1990). *Envisioning Information*. Cheshire, Conn., Graphics Press.

UHLIG, CLAUS (1990). 'Tradition in Curtius and Eliot.' *Comparative Literature*, 42: 193–207.

ULLMANN, MANFRED (1972). *Die Natur- und Geheimwissenschaften im Islam*. Leiden, Brill.

VALE, MALCOLM (1977). *The Cult of Chivalry*. London, Duckworth.

VALENCY, MAURICE JACQUES (1975). *In Praise of Love: An Introduction to the Love-Poetry of the Renaissance* (1958). Repr. New York, Octagon.

VALENTINUS. *See* Basilius Valentinus.

VALERIANO, PIERIO (1613). *Hieroglyphica . . .* (Basle, 1556). Frankfurt.

VASARI, GIORGIO (1901). *Lives of the . . . Painters, Sculptors, and Architects* (1550, 1568). Trans. Mrs Jonathan Foster. 5 vols. Repr. London, Bohn.

VAUGHAN, HENRY (1957). *The Works of Henry Vaughan*. Ed. L. C. Martin. Rev. edn. Oxford, Clarendon Press.

VERDON, TIMOTHY, and HENDERSON, JOHN (1990). *Christianity and the Renaissance: Image and Religious Imagination in the Quattrocento.* Syracuse, NY, Syracuse University Press.

VERGARA, LISA (1982). *Rubens and the Poetics of Landscape.* New Haven, Yale University Press.

VICKERS, BRIAN (1988). 'Rhetoric and Poetics.' In Quentin Skinner *et al.*, eds., *The Cambridge History of Renaissance Philosophy.* Gen. ed. Charles B. Schmitt. Cambridge University Press.

VORAGINE, JACOBUS DE (1900). *The Golden Legend.* Trans. William Caxton. 7 vols. London, Dent.

VREELAND, HAMILTON (1917). *Hugo Grotius, the Father of the Modern Science of International Law.* New York, Oxford University Press.

WALKER, JAMES E. (1895). *The Blessed Dead in Paradise.* Rev. edn. London.

WALTON, IZAAK (1973). *The Lives . . .* Ed. George Saintsbury (1927). London, Oxford University Press.

————— (1983). *The Compleat Angler.* Ed. Jonquil Bevan. Oxford, Clarendon Press.

WALTON, KENDALL L. (1990). *Mimesis as Make-Believe: On the Foundations of the Representational Arts.* Cambridge, Mass.: Harvard University Press.

WATSON, ELIZABETH SEE (1993). *Achille Bocchi and the Emblem Book as Symbolic Form.* Cambridge University Press.

WEBSTER, CHARLES, ed. (1974). *The Intellectual Revolution of the Seventeenth Century.* Past and Present. London, Routledge & Kegan Paul.

————— (1975). *The Great Instauration: Science, Medicine and Reform 1626–1660.* London, Duckworth.

WEISBACH, WERNER (1919). *Trionfi.* Berlin, Grote.

WEITZMANN, KURT (1959). *Ancient Book Illumination.* Martin Classical Lectures 16. Cambridge, Mass., Harvard University Press.

WELU, JAMES A. (1983). *The Collector's Cabinet: Flemish Paintings from New England Private Collections.* Worcester, Mass., Worcester Art Museum.

WENDORF, RICHARD (1990). *The Elements of Life: Biography and Portrait-Painting in Stuart and Georgian England.* Oxford, Clarendon Press.

WESTERWEEL, BART (1983). *Patterns and Patterning: A Study of Four Poems by George Herbert.* Amsterdam, Rodopi.

WESTFALL, RICHARD S. (1973). *Science and Religion in Seventeenth-*

Century England (1958). Repr. Ann Arbor, University of Michigan Press.

WESTFALL, SUZANNE R. (1990). *Patrons and Performance: Early Tudor Household Revels*. Oxford, Clarendon Press.

WESTMAN, ROBERT S., ed. (1975). *The Copernican Achievement*. Berkeley, University of California Press.

WESTRICH, SAL (1992). 'A Coffee for Van Gogh.' *FMR*, No. 58: 20–6.

WHALLON, WILLIAM (1983). *Inconsistencies: Studies in the New Testament, The Inferno, Othello, and Beowulf*. Woodbridge, Brewer.

WHITE, ANDREW D. (1896). *A History of the Warfare of Science with Theology in Christendom*. London.

WHITROW, G. J. (1988). *Time in History: The Evolution of Our General Awareness of Time and Temporal Perspective*. Oxford University Press.

WIECK, ROGER S. (1988). *Time Sanctified: The Book of Hours in Medieval Art and Life*. New York, Braziller for the Walters Art Gallery.

WILKINS, JOHN (1972). *The Discovery of a World in the Moon . . . (1638)*. Facs. Amsterdam, Theatrum Orbis Terrarum.

WILLIAMS, GEORGE HUNTSTON (1962). *The Radical Reformation*. Philadelphia, Westminster Press.

WILLIAMSON, J. W. (1978). *The Myth of the Conqueror: Prince Henry Stuart: A Study in Seventeenth Century Personation*. New York, AMS.

WILLS (*or* Willes), RICHARD (1573). *Poematum Liber*. London.

WILSON, ELKIN CALHOUN (1966). *England's Eliza* (1939). Repr. London, Cass.

WIND, EDGAR (1967). *Pagan Mysteries in the Renaissance*. Rev. edn. London, Faber.

WITHER, GEORGE (1968). *A Collection of Emblems, Ancient and Modern . . .* Facs. Ed. John Horden. Menston, Scolar Press.

WITHINGTON, ROBERT (1963). *English Pageantry: An Historical Outline*. 2 vols. Repr. New York, Blom.

WITTIE, ROBERT (1681). *Ouranoskopia; or, A Survey of the Heavens: A Plain Description of the Admirable Fabric and Motions of the Heavenly Bodies, as they are Discovered to the Eye by the Telescope . . .* London.

WITTKOWER, RUDOLF (1977). *Allegory and the Migration of Symbols*. London, Thames & Hudson.

——— and MARGOT (1963). *Born under Saturn: The Character and Conduct of Artists: A Documented History from Antiquity to the French Revolution*. London, Weidenfeld & Nicolson.

WRIGHT, A. D. (1982). *The Counter-Reformation: Catholic Europe and the Non-Christian World.* New York, St Martin's Press.

WROTH, LADY MARY (1983). *The Poems of Lady Mary Wroth.* Ed. Josephine A. Roberts. Baton Rouge, Louisiana State University Press.

Yale Prose Milton: Don M. Wolfe *et al.*, eds. (1953–82). *The Complete Prose Works of John Milton.* 8 vols. New Haven, Yale University Press.

YATES, FRANCES A. (1966). *The Art of Memory.* London, Routledge.

———— (1969). *Theatre of the World.* London, Routledge.

———— (1975). *Astraea: The Imperial Theme in the Sixteenth Century.* London, Routledge.

———— (1984). *Collected Essays.* iii: *Ideas and Ideals in the North European Renaissance.* London, Routledge.

YOCH, JAMES J. (1978). 'Architecture as Virtue: The Luminous Palace from Homeric Dream to Stuart Propaganda.' *Studies in Philology*, 75: 403–29.

ZAFRAN, ERIC M. (1988). *Fifty Old Master Paintings from the Walters Art Gallery.* Baltimore, Walters Art Gallery.

ZOLLA, ELÉMIRE (1988). 'The Mirror of Cosmic Order.' Trans. Jonathan Keates. *FMR.* No. 32: 58–70.

Index

afterlife: in moon 81; in stars
  61–86, 126–7; in sun 81
Agincourt, Serin d' 4
Al Fargani 40
Alberti, Leon Battista 4, 29,
  29 n. 95
alchemy 79–80, 85
altars 29, 57
Ambrose, Saint 67
Ancients and Moderns 27
Anteros 3
antiquities 5
Arbeau, Thoinot 51
architecture 117–26; pagan façades
  imitated 28; sacrificial
  motifs 29–31
Arcturus 97–8
Ariosto 55
Aristotle 2, 64, 76, 111–12
Arminianism 1, 43
Arthur 93, 96–8, 103; and
  Arcturus 97–8; and Boötes
  97–8; and Corona Borealis 98
Arundel, second earl of 5, 119
Ashmole, Elias 101
Astell, Mary 122 n. 72
Astraea 99–101
astrology 44, 76; see also astronomy,
  constellations, planetary
  systems, signs, zodiac
astronomy, Renaissance 35–58,
  67–70; in America 51; chaotic,
  36; discoveries 25, 44, 58,
  67–8; and encomium 49,
  104; enthusiasm for 44–58; in
  masques 48; Muse of 48;
  poetic simplification 48; princes'
  interest in 41; survival of
  Ptolemaic system 39, 64; see also
  astrology, calendar reform,
  constellations, globe (celestial),
  planetary spheres, planetary
  systems, signs, zodiac
Aubrey, John 118

Augustine, Saint 2, 7, 89,
  109; influence 11, 34
Augustus (Octavianus) 66

Babel, Tower of 113
Bacon, Francis, Viscount St
  Albans 5, 112
Baren, Jan Anton van der 16
Basilius Valentinus 80
Baxter, Richard 24
Beedome, Thomas 78
Belon, Pierre 4
Bevan, Jonquil 61
Bèze, Théodore 94, 110
Boccaccio, Giovanni 88
Bocchi, Achille 23, 94
Boehme, Jakob 17
Bold, Samuel 72, 74
Bongo, Pietro 104
Boria, Juan de 121
Braden, Gordon 89
Brahe, Tycho 41, 45; discovers
  nova 44, 76; epicycles 70; see
  also planetary systems (Tycho's)
Brome, Richard 72
Browne, Sir Thomas 34–5
Browne, William 117
Brueghel, Jan (the younger) 15–16
Bruno, Giordano 42, 102
Burton, Robert 69–70
Bush, Douglas 34
Butler, Martin 102–3

calendar 3, 15 n. 57; reform of 42
Calvin, Jean 11–12, 43
Calvinism 1, 12; and
  Copernicanism 12, 43
Camden, William 5, 45, 101
Campian, Thomas 3 n. 8
Canova 120
Capitol 45, 94–6
Carew, Thomas 30; WORKS: